The Bluebird

A volume in

THE AUDUBON NATURALIST LIBRARY

LAWRENCE ZELENY

✗ ✗ ✗ ✗ ✗

THE BLUEBIRD

How You Can Help

Its Fight

for Survival

Published for the Audubon Naturalist Society
of the Central Atlantic States
by
Indiana University Press
BLOOMINGTON

The kindness of the many people who have helped make this book possible is gratefully acknowledged. In particular I am indebted to George E. Watson and Chandler S. Robbins for professional advice and to George E. Watson and David Krieg for their painstaking reviews and improvement of the manuscript. Inestimable contributions have also been made by the hundreds of persons throughout the United States and Canada who have shared their bluebird experiences with me. These valuable contacts were for the most part made possible by Tom Coulson through the medium of the *Purple Martin News*.

Special thanks go to the following for their permission to reproduce many of the photographs included in the book: Gregory Cramer, Jack R. Finch, Joseph F. Huber, Fred Lahrman, Hubert W. Prescott, Dickson Preston, Lorne Scott, and Michael L. Smith; to Jack Schroeder for the drawing that graces the chapter opening pages; and to Nancy E. MacClintock for her great efficiency in preparing the index (not to mention her enthusiasm for the bluebird conservation cause).

Manufactured in the United States of America

Library of Congress Cataloging in Publication Data

Zeleny, Lawrence, 1904–
   The bluebird.

   (The Audubon naturalist library)
   Bibliography
   Includes index.
      1. Bluebirds—United States.   2. Rare birds.
   I. Title. II. Series.
   QL696.P288Z44   1976   598.8'42   74-22832
   cl. ISBN 0-253-10750-4
   pa. ISBN 0-253-20212-4   5 6 7 85 84 83

To OLIVE

*who shares my deep love of nature and has encouraged and
assisted me in writing this book, and who is largely
responsible for the wonderful experiences related in
Chapter 11. She and I first met many years ago in the late
Dr. Thomas S. Roberts' ornithology class at the
University of Minnesota, where we
fell in love with birds and with each other.*

Contents

Illustrations

COLOR PLATES
(following page 26)

FIGURES

FOREWORD

WITH THIS BOOK, the Audubon Naturalist Society of the Central Atlantic States inaugurates a new series of publications, the "Audubon Naturalist Library," on the natural history and conservation of the plants and animals indigenous to the central Atlantic region. The book's theme—how we can ensure that there will be bluebirds for posterity—is a fitting message in the year 1976, directly in keeping with the Society's own Bicentennial focus on celebrating our country's rich natural heritage, particularly our wildlife heritage.

Publication enables an organization to share the fruits of its labor with the public at large, and the Audubon Naturalist Society is proud of its long publishing record. As president, I take pleasure in seeing the Society launch this exciting new series in the Bicentennial year with an outstanding and timely book. Lawrence Zeleny's *The Bluebird: How You Can Help Its Fight for Survival* is a milestone of another sort as well: it is the Society's first venture into full-color illustration in its more than 75 years of existence.

The story of the bluebird is a dramatic story of struggle

for survival. Happily, it is also a story of hope and inspiration that should inspire all Americans who care about their
natural heritage to increase their understanding of ecology
and redouble their conservation efforts. Inspiration is the
beginning of discovery. The wilderness dies when the sense
of discovery dies. True naturalists see facts as phenomena
and contemplate mechanisms with wonder and romance.
Our author is a naturalist in the best sense, one who keeps
alive the sense of discovery and thus the sense of wilderness
at your doorstep.

The story told within these pages is far more than a story
of a species of bird. It is the odyssey of one man, a gentle
and learned man, in lifelong dedication to a cause—a crusade
to rescue a species in nature from the threshold of doom. A
layman's ode to environmental concern, it is a testament to
the communion of amateur and professional in the struggle
to preserve the quality of our natural estate. It also is a blue-
print for the practical union of natural history and conservation, and a primer for grassroots action. Natural history
studies are the beginning of wisdom in all environmental
matters. Zeleny's book embodies the spirit of popular natural
history study, the ever-growing national pastime epito-
mized by the 75-year-old Audubon movement.

The bluebird ought to be America's national bird, and
I hope this book will start a groundswell for its election.
What species could better symbolize the pristine beauty of
the American wilderness as our forefathers found it, or the
idealism and wholesomeness of the American experience?
Few birds are so widely native throughout the quarters of
the continent, few are so well known, and perhaps none is
so guileless. Few birds evoke such nostalgia for childhood,
memories of old-fashioned spring mornings in the country
or down on Grandma's farm. For those who were young

when bluebirds still flourished, the memory of a bluebird's predawn warble or of a glimpse of a sun-bathed flash of pure blue lives forever. The bluebird, instantly winsome to young and old alike and to people of modern or traditional sensibilities alike, is American idealism personified—a flying piece of sky, a living poem, a crystal note, an emblem of nature's moral conscience. Today millions of Americans yearn for the warm reassurance long associated with the nation's rural environment, and the mere sight of a bluebird can evoke that warmth and reassurance. Fortunately, the hour is not too late for something to be done to help the bluebird's fight for survival. Save-the-bluebird fan clubs have sprung up everywhere recently, and we must hope that the bluebird's return has only begun.

The name of John James Audubon (who was born scarcely ten years after the signing of the Declaration of Independence) has come to symbolize popular interest in the study and preservation of nature, especially of birdlife. More than anyone in his own time, and perhaps in all time, Audubon made known the richness of the birds of America and set the stage for environmental concern. Today we know, after many costly lessons, that the ecological web is all-encompassing and that only a few short links in the food chain separate Audubon's birds from everyman's biosphere. Audubon represents the innocent beginnings of conservation in America. In the nearly 200 years since his birth interest in conservation has matured into an all-encompassing crusade to save our environment. The "Audubon movement," by whatever name it may go, has never ceased to grow, to expand its influence, and to increase its comprehension of nature. Yet the movement will always be rooted in basic natural history and the timeless principle of learning about nature from nature itself. Thanks to this movement, old-fashioned natural history is not dead. Zeleny's book exemplifies the crucial role that the Audubon and other popular societies have played for a long time in the transfer of knowledge from the establishment of science to the ranks of the people.

The Audubon Naturalist Society, founded in 1897, was one of the very first groups to invoke the good name and good work of Audubon to rally the public to the cause of conservation. For more than three-quarters of a century, it has been teaching natural history and preaching environmental concern. The Society also was among the first to take an ecological and biospheric approach to natural history education. After World War II, with Rachel Carson as an active member, the Society pioneered in pointing out the hazards posed by indiscriminate use of pesticides. Today the Society's far-flung activities include the on-going Bald Eagle Survey and the Bluebird project, the latter directed by Zeleny in concert with many other individuals and groups across the country.

In George Watson's Introduction the reader will find a detailed account of the background and purpose of this book. Dr. Watson is a distinguished ornithologist who has long been an active member of the Audubon Naturalist Society and has served the Society in several important capacities. It was during his recent tenure as Vice President for Publications that the plan for this book was conceived and then developed to the point of fruition. The Society is greatly indebted to him for the vital role that he has played. As for the author, words cannot express our profound appreciation for Larry Zeleny's selfless dedication and generosity in preparing this manuscript for publication under the auspices of the Society, with the proceeds to go toward the furtherance of the Society's efforts in conservation and education.

Today countless people, especially in urban America, are tiring of the synthetic biomes of our manmade estate. If they could make one Bicentennial wish, it might well be for an authentic glimpse of Audubon's wilderness, the wilderness of our founding fathers. The bluebird story, told so earnestly and delightfully by Larry Zeleny, offers just such a glimpse. In truth, much of Audubon's wilderness is still with us on the occasion of our 200th birthday, thanks in significant measure to the Audubon movement. We must make the most of this good fortune by supporting such positive and successful restoration efforts as those set forth in this book.

December 12, 1975   STANWYN G. SHETLER
President, Audubon Naturalist Society
of the Central Atlantic States, Inc.

INTRODUCTION

WHEN I WAS A BOY in southern Connecticut over 30 years ago, I used to delight in watching a male eastern bluebird in a neighbor's old apple orchard. I was thrilled to see its vivid blue back as it sat on a low branch near its nest hole. And I still get excited whenever I see a bluebird. My first look into a bluebird's nesting box, however, was a disappointment. Another neighbor had a sturdy nesting box on his back porch, which early in the season had been frequented by a pair of bluebirds. A pair of house wrens soon took over and signalled their tenancy by narrowing the entrance with a baffle of twigs. At the end of the summer when we opened the box to clean it out for the next year's tenants, the fate of the bluebirds' attempt at raising a family was clear. Beneath the wrens' heap of sticks was a neat grass cup. As I separated the wren and bluebird layers I found four pale azure bluebird eggs, each neatly punctured. Here was natural competition for nest sites. The mild-mannered bluebirds had lost to the aggressive wrens in this particular instance, perhaps because the backyard habitat had favored the wrens. But bluebirds obviously have coexisted with wrens in America for thousands of years. Indeed, when the European colonists began clearing the virgin forest along the east coast for their farms, bluebirds, along with other open habitat species, undoubtedly became more abundant and flourished.

In 1851 and 1890, however, two events took place that promised to cause grief to our beautiful and confiding native bluebird. Along with the flood of 19th-century human immigrants that strengthened our country came two avian immigrants eager to make their fortune in the New World: house sparrows and starlings. Each was adapted to the crowded urban and suburban environments of industrial Germany and England and at least one—the sparrow—already had a great track record for spreading. For a while after the first landing on the eastern seaboard, the house sparrow and the starling stayed close to home, but within a few years of their introduction each had begun to mulitply and spread. These resourceful urban immigrants were also adapted to living in rural farmland. Each liked to have a roof over its head and that's why they eventually started putting pressure on bluebirds, and to a lesser degree on some of our other hole- or cavity-nesting native species.

The sparrows, true to their weaver ancestry, were highly social and stayed in flocks both for feeding and to some extent for nesting. The starlings, too, were gregarious, at least for feeding and roosting. Not only did both species take over rafters in barns and nooks about houses, but they inspected and adopted the nesting boxes that bluebird lovers had just begun to put up for bluebirds in the late 19th century, and even invaded hollow trees in orchards along woodland edges and hollow fenceposts in pastureland. Bluebird nest sites have also grown scarcer in recent years because farmers have manicured their orchards by pruning low-hanging hollow limbs and because some farmers have replaced wooden fenceposts, which rotted quickly and provided cozy hollows for bluebirds in colonial days, with metal or concrete posts.

In the 1930's and 1940's bird watchers began to ask "Where are all those gentle bluebirds I knew 30 years ago?" And some, like Larry Zeleny, Seth Low, Tom Musselman, Amelia Laskey and John Lane had already begun to study the situation and do something about it. Larry's first observations of bluebird nesting began in Minnesota in 1919. He and others started measuring bluebird nest holes and waist sizes, and investigated the location of successful nests and the role of predators and competitors. They concluded that only through a massive saturation of suitable open pastureland, manicured orchards and suburban backyards with scientifically designed predator- and competitor-proof nesting boxes could they halt the bluebird population decline. They later established and carefully monitored bluebird trails with tens, hundreds, and in recent years thousands of nesting boxes, and set up communication networks by mail, newspaper columns, and magazine articles.

Wherever there were trail sponsors, bluebirds began to reappear for people to enjoy. I know my own thrill when driving through Beltsville, Maryland, today in seeing a bluebird sitting on a fence post near one of Larry Zeleny's rectangular nesting boxes. It isn't quite the same thrill of discovery that I experienced as an eleven-year-old boy when I saw my first bluebird, but it is nevertheless a very exciting experience, especially when I think of the odds against these gentle birds.

We'll never be able to rid this country of our feathered European immigrants, and some have even suggested that our native bald eagle, which also appears to be losing its fight for survival in most of the United States, ought to be replaced as the national bird by one of our major immigrant species. The feisty sparrow and strutting starling, they argue, are more representative of our national spirit. But as Larry Zeleny and other bluebird conservationists have proved, it needn't be inevitable that the bluebirds go on endlessly losing ground to the alien species. European man transplanted to the New World has tipped the scales against some of the native American species. Now it is time for us to try to counterbalance the scale in favor of the bluebird.

This is a job that amateurs—in both its senses, that is, non-professionals and lovers—can best accomplish. Bluebird amateurs abound in the United States and Canada and their nesting box trails form a network of hope across our great continent. True, some professionals such as Seth Low, David Kreig, and Benedict Pinkowski have made significant contributions in their carefully documented studies of bluebird food habits, habitat preferences, and behavior, which will be of great use in bluebird conservation and recovery. But it is the organized army of bluebird trail tenders and box erectors who will put the professionals' scientific knowledge into practice to bring the bluebird back to our yards, orchards, and pastures.

Larry Zeleny is one of the leaders and major missionaries of this active conservation movement. He has spearheaded the Audubon Naturalist Society's campaign for bluebird conservation. His nesting box design was adopted by the Society for distribution through its bookstore, and his blue-bird column and reports appear regularly in the Society's publications, the *Audubon Naturalist News* and the *Atlantic Naturalist*.

In his 56-year-long mission of love, Larry has had many rewarding experiences with people and birds alike. He has built up a vast correspondence with other bluebird conservationists with whom he can share his knowledge. But even more rewarding has been his friendship with the confiding bluebirds themselves. His account of rearing a pair of orphaned bluebirds and of watching his foster children produce a new generation of bluebirds is truly a remarkable story of the bond between suburban man and nature. Larry's experience leads one to think that the bluebirds show many human attributes. One of his remarkable discoveries was that two young males from a first brood helped their widowed father feed their younger second brood siblings after their mother died. Such apparent altruistic behavior of "helpers-at-the-nest" is a current topic of field and theoretical research by behaviorists, ecologists, and evolutionists. Larry's observations, along with a few scattered reports since 1931 and another that has just appeared in *The Auk*, suggest that the bluebird could well become a classic example of brood altruism, a fascinating possibility that should entice new researchers to turn their attention to bluebirds.

Larry Zeleny's story of what a vast army of amateur conservationists have done and can do to help our bluebirds should serve as inspiring example for other conservationists in the constant battle to help our wildlife survive in an increasingly technological and hostile environment.

November 14, 1975

GEORGE E. WATSON
Curator of Birds
National Museum of Natural History
Smithsonian Institution

The Bluebird

... when the last individual of a race
of living things breathes no more,
another heaven and another earth must pass
before such a one can be again.

WILLIAM BEEBE

[1]
Why the Special Concern for Bluebirds?

THE BLUEBIRD has long been one of the best loved North American birds, not only because of its gorgeous coloring but also for its gentle disposition and the tender beauty of its voice at all seasons of the year. No bird has been mentioned so frequently in the lyrics of our songs, and the bluebird occupies a special place in American prose and poetry as well as in song as a symbol of love, hope, and happiness. To those who know it well the bluebird seems capable of expressing almost every conceivable human mood and emotion. The late Frank M. Chapman of the American Museum of Natural History, one of America's foremost ornithologists, was moved to express his feelings poetically in his classic *Birds of Eastern North America:*

> The Bluebird's disposition is typical of all that is sweet and amiable. His song breathes of love; even his fall call-note—*tur-wee, tur-wee*—is soft and gentle. So associated is his voice with the birth and death of the seasons that to me his

song is freighted with all the gladness of springtime, while the sad notes of the birds passing southward tell me more plainly than the falling leaves that the year is dying.

The early settlers in colonial times looked upon the bluebird as the true harbinger of spring and fondly called it the "blue robin" since its colors reminded them somewhat of their beloved robin in Europe.

Those of us who were enjoying birds half a century and more ago will recall that the bluebird was one of our commonest birds and that it nested freely close to human habitations, even in the residential sections of large cities. But now few people under twenty or thirty years of age, especially those who live east of the Rockies, can recall ever having seen a bluebird. To some, indeed, it must seem a bird that lives only in the fancy of poets and songwriters, a mythical creation that combines all of the most appealing avian traits.

It is sad indeed that this wonderful bird has now disappeared almost entirely from urban and suburban communities and that even in most rural areas it has become so scarce that only ardent bird watchers are likely to be aware of its presence. Although no accurate population figures are available, a reasonable estimate is that during the course of the last forty years the population of the eastern bluebird (one of the three recognized bluebird species) may have dropped by as much as 90 percent or more. If this relentless rate of decline continues it is quite conceivable that the eastern bluebird will disappear completely, never to return, within the foreseeable future. Although the mountain and western species of bluebirds have not yet been so drastically affected, they too are withdrawing steadily in the face of a changing environment, and it may be but a matter of time before the sighting of a bluebird will be a pleasure reserved only for those who are hardy enough to venture into the most remote areas of the country.

Fortunately, the causes of the decline in the bluebird population now seem to be fairly well understood, and there is good evidence that with coordinated efforts on the part of individuals and groups concerned about the bluebirds' fate, it would be possible to halt and, it is hoped, even to reverse this decline. In writing this book I have tried to tell a bit about the life history of these birds, to alert my readers to the serious problems they now face, and to explain what can be done to aid them in their desperate struggle for survival. If this little book succeeds in its purpose, you and your children, and your children's children, will enjoy a world made richer by the continued presence of these beautiful and fascinating birds.

[2]

Bluebirds and Their Behavior

BLUEBIRDS are distinctive in both appearance and behavior. They are one of the few North American birds that are primarily blue in color, and they belong to the relatively small group of native cavity-nesting species. For a full understanding of why these birds have such popular appeal and an appreciation of the dangers that they face, some knowledge of their habits and lifestyle is helpful.

Bluebird Species

The thrush family, Turdidae, to which the bluebirds belong, consists of some six hundred species distributed widely throughout most of the world. Thrushes in general are noted for the exquisite sweetness and expressiveness of their songs, the North American hermit and wood thrushes in particular being considered among the most appealing of all bird songsters. Bluebirds, whose song has been described as a pure contralto, are found only in North America. At least one of the three species may be found in every state except Hawaii, as well as in most of Canada and parts of Mexico.

The eastern bluebird (*Sialia sialis*) breeds in all states and provinces (except Newfoundland) east of the Rocky Mountains. In this species, the male bird's head, back, wings, and tail are a strikingly bright blue. Its throat, breast, and sides are rusty red and the belly is white. The female eastern bluebird resembles the male but is much duller and grayer.

The western bluebird (*Sialia mexicana*) breeds in the western part of the continent from southern Canada south into Mexico and east to Utah and Colorado. The species resembles the eastern bluebird except that its throat is blue and the rusty color of its breast and sides extends over its upper back.

The mountain bluebird (*Sialia currucoides*) breeds throughout most of the northern half of the range of the western bluebird and extends its range east to Manitoba and the Dakotas, and north through western Canada into east-central Alaska. As its name suggests, the mountain bluebird favors high elevations, often being found at altitudes of up to twelve thousand feet. In many places, however, this bird seems equally at home at low altitudes. The male mountain bluebird is entirely blue except for its white belly. The female is mostly gray, showing perceptible blue only on its wings and tail.

The young of all three species before their first fall molts have speckled breasts, a characteristic of most thrushes. Only faint traces of the rusty red coloration of the eastern and western bluebirds are apparent in the juveniles. The sex of juvenile bluebirds can often, but not always, be judged as early as the twelfth day after hatching by the depth of the blue color in the wings and tail. (More detailed criteria for determining the sex of bluebird nestlings have been presented by Pinkowski [1974].)

The approximate breeding ranges of the three species of bluebirds are shown in Fig. 1. Hybridization between mountain and eastern bluebirds (first reported by Lane [1968, 1969]) occurs in areas where the breeding ranges of the two species overlap.

All three species of bluebirds are closely related and their habits are rather similar. They are all faced to somewhat different degrees with the same survival problems resulting from environmental changes brought about directly or indirectly by the hand of man.

Food Habits

Bluebirds are primarily insectivorous, two-thirds or more of their food consisting of a wide variety of insects. Included in their diet are large numbers of insects considered harmful to man. In the spring the bluebirds seem to have a particular fondness for the cutworms that are often ruinous to crops and gardens. Later in the summer and well into the autumn grasshoppers and other *Orthoptera* are consumed in enormous quantities. In fact, grasshoppers, when available, appear to be one of the principal foods of all three species of bluebird.

In obtaining their insect food bluebirds characteristi-

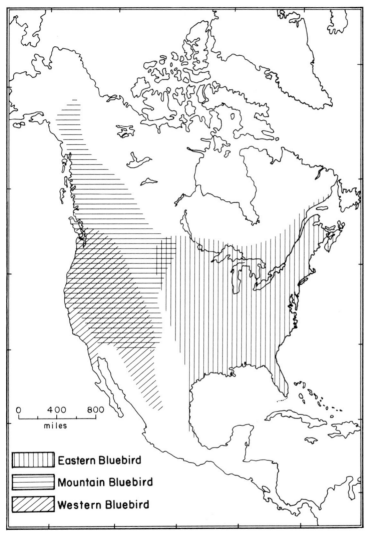

1. Approximate Bluebird Breeding Ranges

Eastern Bluebird

Mountain Bluebird

Western Bluebird

0   400   800
miles

cally sit quietly on an exposed perch, such as a low branch of a tree, a post, or a wire, and scan the ground from that vantage point. Having once spotted a likely prey, they then dart quickly to the ground and return with it to the original or a similar nearby perch. Where suitable lookout perches are not available bluebirds frequently hover over the ground fluttering their wings rapidly (somewhat in the manner of kestrels) while scanning the area for food. The latter method of locating food is especially characteristic of mountain bluebirds.

Less frequently, bluebirds may be seen darting after and seizing flying insects on the wing, in the manner of flycatchers. Although they are not nearly as adept and graceful as New World flycatchers (Tyrannidae) at this kind of maneuver, they nevertheless usually succeed in catching their prey. Surprisingly, young bluebirds that have only recently been fledged often choose this seemingly difficult procedure in their early attempts to obtain their own food. Their efforts are comical to watch, but the experience no doubt hastens their mastery of the art of flying.

In late summer and autumn bluebirds supplement their insect diet with berries—mostly wild varieties, since their taste for fruit usually does not develop until after the cultivated berry season is past. Bluebirds rarely, if ever, do any significant damage to cultivated crops.

In winter, when insects become scarce or unavailable in most parts of their range, bluebirds subsist almost entirely on wild berries of many kinds. They often starve if the wild berry supply becomes exhausted or is covered over by snow or ice.

Courtship

Those fortunate people who have bluebirds nesting close to their homes may have the rare opportunity to observe one of the most beautiful and appealing events in nature, bluebird courtship. Many species of birds exhibit strange and often amazing behavior during courtship. They may strut, dance, scream, grunt, spread their feathers in grotesque displays, inflate bright-colored pouches, or perform almost unbelievable aerial acrobatics. Bluebird courtship has none of these spectacular features but is a thing of gentle beauty.

Bluebird courtship behavior is not as stereotyped as that of many species and may vary considerably according to circumstances. In the case of the eastern bluebird, those birds that remain in their breeding areas throughout the year tend to be less demonstrative during courtship than the more northern members of the species which return to their breeding areas in early spring after wintering in the South. The male birds generally return to their summer homes a few days in advance of the females.

Since bluebirds nest in cavities their courtship activities tend to center around natural holes or nesting boxes and are intimately involved with the selection of sites for their nests.

The male, often after a long search, finds an unoccupied cavity or nesting box that he considers to be a suitable place for his mate to build a nest. His prospective mate is likely to be in the same general area but has usually taken little, if any, active part in the search for a home. His task now, therefore, is to convince her that he has made a wise choice in selecting a nesting site and to entice her into accepting it—which of course would include accepting him as her mate.

To the casual observer the bluebird is no accomplished songster. In fact the songs of the western and mountain bluebirds are rarely heard except by those intrepid listeners who may be out birding before dawn. The eastern bluebird is much more vocal although its best efforts are reserved for the brief courting season. At all times, however, the frequent gentle warbling of both sexes is most pleasing to the human ear. This warbling can be varied ever so slightly, seeming to express every conceivable mood or emotion including love, contentment, fear, rage, and sadness. In the words of Ruth Thomas: "Several other birds sing plaintive or wistful songs, but the Bluebird's warble is sometimes a yearning, other times an all but unbearable ecstasy!"

The eastern bluebird's song is one of love and persuasion as he tries to entice his prospective mate into accepting him and his chosen home. He may interrupt his singing occasionally to bring her a choice caterpillar which she passively accepts. It is hard to understand her apparent indifference at first as she sits quietly on a nearby branch or fence post listening to his passionate appeal and watching him pop in and out of his doorway obviously imploring her to try it herself. One wonders if she is really as indifferent as she pretends to be, or whether she is simply enjoying the show and trying to prolong it as long as possible!

This phase of the courtship may last an hour, a day, or even a week depending largely on how well the female is able to resist the entreaties of the male. During this period his hope and enthusiasm never wane. At last she will probably relent, fly to the cavity or nesting box, and examine it inside and out, speculating as to its suitability. This simple act of hers is evidently interpreted by the male as an outright acceptance of his proposal. His emotion then knows no bounds, his wings quiver with excitement, and his soft but beautiful love song swells in a great crescendo and is embellished with wild new notes of pure joy and unrestrained passion. His exquisite rhapsody is often sung on the wing as he flutters fitfully in circles around the lovely mate who has just accepted him. This is the song that Ruth Thomas so aptly called "an all but unbearable ecstasy".

At times this display is marred briefly by a second male bluebird appearing on the scene with the evident intent of taking over the cavity or nesting box and with it, if possible, the first male's prospective mate. The intruder is usually banished, but sometimes not before a furious battle is fought.

Less frequently a second female bluebird will show up, evidently entranced by the appealing love song of the male. Such an intrusion is not tolerated by the first female and the fury of the ensuing battle may even exceed that of two battling males. The two females will often fall to the ground and roll over and over, each tearing savagely at the other in uncontrolled frenzy. The male will usually watch the struggle in apparent bewilderment and perhaps even with a degree of smug satisfaction that two beautiful females would compete so violently for his attention. If the fight gets too savage, however, he will interfere and with skillful physical force separate the two participants who will fly off in different directions. The battle is usually quickly resumed and continued until one of the participants is banished.

I have been told that on rare occasions a struggle of this kind between two female bluebirds may be settled amicably with the male accepting both birds. In this event he would need to locate quickly a second cavity or nesting box nearby so that each female could build her own nest and pretend that her rival does not exist. Such an arrangement would require considerable finesse and diplomacy on the part of the male. However, this may explain some of the rather rare occurrences reported where two broods of bluebirds are raised at the same time within 50 or 100 feet of each other. Polygamy is common among some birds but seems to be rare among bluebirds if in fact it ever occurs.

To witness a bluebird courtship in early spring is well worth watching and waiting for. It contains all of the elements of tenderness, love, and devotion of the finest human relationship.

Nesting and Care of Young

SELECTION OF THE NESTING SITE

The male bluebird has the responsibility for locating a suitable cavity for the nesting site, but his selection is always subject to the approval of his mate. If she rejects his choice, the male must continue the search until he finds a site acceptable to the female bird. This search for a good nesting site is usually the first order of business when the birds return to their nesting areas in late winter or early spring. Once a site has been selected the pair generally remains in the vicinity until they are ready to build the nest, defending the chosen spot against any competitors that may arrive on the scene. In those rare instances when the number of unoccupied cavities or nesting boxes exceeds the local demand, bluebirds may investigate a number of sites at their leisure before settling on one. Even then the female bluebird may start a nest in one cavity only to abandon it in favor of another. With the steady depletion of good bluebird nesting sites as man's dominion spreads, the opportunities for such choosiness are becoming relatively rare.

As much as six weeks or as little as an hour or even less may elapse between the selection of a nesting site and the beginning of nest building. The interval seems to depend largely on how much difficulty the birds have had in locating and holding a suitable site.

Strangely enough, very short holding periods (i.e., periods during which a pair of birds have taken possession of a site but have not yet begun to build a nest in it) may occur under diametrically opposed sets of circumstances: when available nesting sites are so scarce that the bluebirds are unable to locate one until the time for nest building is already at hand; and when sites are so plentiful that the birds have no need to make an early decision. Long holding periods commonly occur when good sites are scarce but the birds are lucky enough to find one early in their search. Their behavior in such cases clearly suggests that they sense the importance of holding on to their hard-to-find homes until the time comes for nest building.

NEST BUILDING

Nest building is performed almost exclusively by the female bluebird, although the male may occasionally supply a small portion of the nesting material. Most of the male bird's time is given over to encouraging his mate in her work by accompanying her and by warbling softly to her while she gathers nesting material.

Bluebird nests are neatly constructed and are usually rather homogeneous in composition, dry grass being the most common material used when it is available. Relatively little effort is made to line the nest with finer or softer material. Near a pine woods the nests may be made almost entirely of dry pine needles. Other plant materials may be used according to their local availability. Feathers are not commonly used in bluebird nests.

The nest is usually about three or four inches deep, even though the cavity or nesting box in which it is situated may be much deeper. Sometimes, however, the nest may be built up much higher so that its upper rim is only slightly below the entrance hole. The cup of the nest (i.e. the depression into which the eggs are deposited) is approximately $2\frac{3}{8}''$ in diameter and 2 or $2\frac{1}{2}$ inches deep when the nest is first constructed.

Nest building for the first brood usually starts by mid March in the far south, by early April in the middle latitudes of the U.S., and by late April or early May in the northern states and in Canada. Cold or unusually wet weather may delay its start. The actual time of the start of nest building may also vary considerably among individual pairs of bluebirds in a given locality. Late nesting often results from the inability of the birds to find suitable sites early enough or from their having been driven out of previously selected sites.

Bluebirds typically require five or six days to complete a nest once they have begun, but may take as long as two weeks or more. On occasion a bluebird will build an entire nest in only a day or two to ensure that it will be ready for eggs that are about to be laid. In one case that I observed, a pair of bluebirds were driven from their newly built nest by house sparrows before any eggs had been laid. The eviction occurred at a most inopportune time, for the female bluebird was nearly ready to lay her first egg. The bluebirds seemed to sense the urgency of the situation, quickly took possession of a nearby vacant nesting box, and worked frantically to build a new nest. It was completed and the first egg laid all within a single day. Not surprisingly, this "emergency" nest was rather shallow and lacked the fine skill and workmanship characteristic of bluebird nests constructed in a more leisurely fashion.

EGG LAYING

Egg laying ordinarily starts soon after the nest is finished, but again, there may be considerable variation and the first egg may not be laid for a week or more. A single egg is laid each day, usually in the morning, until the clutch is complete. The eastern bluebird usually lays from three to five eggs, occasionally six, and on rare occasions as few as two or as many as seven. The average number of eggs in the clutch is slightly higher for the western and mountain bluebirds, particularly for the latter species, which sometimes lays as many as eight eggs. Probably the largest number of bluebird eggs ever found in one nest was a clutch of nine mountain bluebird eggs (of which eight eventually hatched) reported by Scott [1974] near Indian Head, Saskatchewan, in June, 1973. The number of eggs in the second and third broods of the season tends to be slightly lower than for the first brood.

Bluebird eggs are approximately 21 millimeters long and 16 millimeters wide at their broadest point. The eggs of the mountain bluebird are on the average very slightly larger than those of the other two species. The eggs of all three species are normally a clear blue with no markings whatever, although an occasional bluebird lays pure white eggs.

INCUBATION

Like most other songbirds, bluebirds usually do not start incubating until the last egg of the clutch is laid. This ensures that all of the young birds will be approximately the same size and age. Thus they can compete on even terms for the food supplied by the parent birds.

Incubation, like nest building, is performed almost exclusively by the female bluebird. The male sometimes stays in the nesting cavity while the female is out, but it is doubtful that he contributes much to the incubation of the eggs. The male usually remains in the vicinity of the nest throughout the incubation period and is ready to defend the nest against intruders. The male bird also supplies the female with occasional insects while she is on the nest, but this seems to be more a token of his devotion than a significant source of the female's nourishment. She leaves the nest often enough to obtain most of her own food, and if necessary, all of it. On warm, sunny days she seems to sense that her eggs will keep warm for a considerable length of time without her attention, and she may remain away for an hour or more at a time. On cold days, however, she will leave the nest only for brief periods. Incubation continues throughout the night regardless of the weather.

The incubation period for bluebird eggs is usually either thirteen or fourteen days, although occasional periods as short as twelve days or as long as sixteen have been noted, and one observer (Pinkowski [1974]) reported an exceptionally long incubation of twenty-one days, during which period the weather was quite cold and the female seemed rather negligent in her task of keeping her eggs warm. The fourteen-day incubation period seems common for first broods, and the thirteen-day period for the second and third broods. The higher temperatures of the summer months may hasten the incubation of the later broods slightly.

As soon as the eggs hatch the female bluebird removes the shells from the nest and carries them a considerable distance away, presumably to avoid leaving any clue that would assist predators in finding her nest. She may also eat part of the shells, which would help supply the calcium needed in her diet.

CARE OF THE YOUNG

The parents share about equally in the task of feeding the nestlings. For the first few days the nestlings are fed small, soft insects of various kinds; but before they are ready to leave the nest their food includes such seemingly indigestible fare as grasshoppers and hard-shelled beetles. A few wild berries are sometimes added to the diet, particularly for the later broods. Food is brought to the brood at an average rate of once about every five minutes from dawn to dusk. In this way each nestling in a brood of four is fed at roughly twenty minute intervals. Occasionally young bluebirds of an earlier brood assist their parents in feeding the nestlings of subsequent broods.

The parents and any young birds that may be assisting in feeding the nestlings keep the nest clean by removing the fecal sacs and depositing them a considerable distance away (again, presumably in order not to betray the nest's location to any would-be predators). The fecal sacs consist of thin membranes containing fecal matter, and they usually remain intact so that the birds can carry them away with little soiling.

The nestlings are brooded by the mother bird much of the time, including the entire nighttime, for the first few days, since they are practically naked and unable to generate their own body heat. Later, when feather growth has commenced, they are brooded more sporadically, and for several days before they leave the nest they are not brooded at all. How much brooding takes place depends somewhat on the weather, more brooding being done during cold weather, for obvious reasons.

2. Bluebird nest with eggs

(Photo by Lorne Scott)

3. Mountain bluebird on a nest

(Photo by Michael L. Smith)

(Photo by Michael L. Smith)

4. Female eastern bluebird bringing food to the nest

5. Female eastern bluebird feeding her young

(Photo by Gregory Cramer)

(Photo by Fred Lahrman)

6. Mountain bluebird nestlings

7. Fledgling eastern bluebird

The baby birds grow at a remarkable rate, and in the case of the eastern bluebird are ready to leave the nest within fifteen to twenty days after hatching. In the great majority of instances they depart on the seventeenth or eighteenth day. It has been reported (Power [1966]) that mountain bluebirds usually leave the nest twenty-two or twenty-three days after hatching. How long the nestlings remain in the nest probably depends to some degree on the food supply, which naturally affects the rate of growth. Weather is also a factor. In a cold, rainy spell the nestlings may delay fledging until the weather improves. Nest sanitation is often neglected on the last day the young birds are in the nest.

When the young birds first leave the opening of the nesting cavity or box they attempt to fly directly to the nearest tree, shrub, fence, or any other point where they can alight some distance off the ground. They are usually strong enough to fly from fifty to one hundred feet on the first attempt. I once witnessed the maiden flight of a young bluebird that flew more than seven hundred feet to the nearest tree, with the aid of a strong tail wind!

This ability of young birds to fly at the time of leaving the nest is common among cavity-nesting birds, but much less common among birds that build their nests in the open. Young robins, for example, usually flutter to the ground on first leaving their nests and are not able to fly any appreciable distance for a day or more. Consequently robin fledglings suffer a much higher casualty rate from predators than do bluebird fledglings.

Shortly after their first flight young bluebirds work their way by means of short flights and hops up into the higher branches of nearby trees. They usually remain well up off the ground for several days, flying from tree to tree while they gain strength and perfect their flying skill. While thus reveling in their newly discovered surroundings they keep one another and the adult birds constantly informed of their whereabouts by means of plaintive call notes. The parents, sometimes with assistance from young birds of an earlier brood, continue to feed the fledglings since they are as yet unable to find their own food. At night and often on rainy days the newly fledged bluebirds huddle closely together on a branch, presumably for warmth and companionship.

Except for the last brood of the season the mother

bird usually stops feeding the young birds within a week or ten days after they are fledged, sometimes sooner. She then devotes her time to building a new nest in preparation for another brood, leaving the care of the previous brood to their father. The young birds begin finding some part of their own food when they have been out of the nest for about two weeks. This appears to be encouraged by the male parent who at about that time starts a "weaning" process. In another week or ten days the young birds have learned to find all of their own food, and thus are no longer dependent upon their parents or older siblings.

The hazards of bluebird existence are considerable, and it is not uncommon for one of the adult birds to perish during the nesting period. What then happens to the eggs or young birds remaining in the nest? Enough observations have been made of situations of this kind to supply some of the answers.

If the male bluebird dies while the female is incubating the eggs, the female may desert her nest. But there is a good chance she will remain instead and continue to incubate and then to raise her brood alone. The widowed mother must then work very hard indeed, for she must supply about twice as much food as she would have to with the help of a mate. Unless the brood is a large one and the weather is unfavorable to insects, the female bluebird usually proves capable of carrying out this difficult task. If the brood is the second or third of the season one or more of the young birds of an earlier brood may help with the feeding of the current brood. Such assistance in the feeding and care of younger siblings is relatively rare in the bird world, and appears to be more common among bluebirds than among most other species. In many ways bluebirds appear to have remarkably strong family ties and what in human terms would be thought of as a sense of family loyalty. If the weather is cold and wet, insects may be scarce and a bit of discreet human assistance might be beneficial, especially if the widowed female is receiving no help from others of her kind. Small amounts of canned dog food, ground beef, or small pieces of hard-boiled egg yolk (all rich in the protein that is essential to a bluebird's diet) may be left in a conspicuous spot near the nest—but should never be put in the nest itself. One should not attempt to feed the nestlings directly as the mother bird is much more skilled at this task.

A few years ago I made frequent observations of a brood of bluebird nestlings which had lost its father. The brood was being well fed and cared for by three female birds, two adults and one immature, presumably the actual mother, an unmated adult female, and an immature female of an earlier brood. The three birds carried out their domestic duties in complete harmony. They were frequently seen sitting together on a fence near the nest, each with an insect in its bill, carrying on friendly bluebird "conversation." They took turns feeding the nestlings and removing fecal sacs from the nest. The widowed mother bird, thanks to this cooperative relationship, was not overworked, and the nestlings were fledged on schedule in perfect health. This kind of cooperation involving birds other than the true parents—technically known as altruistic behavior—is very imperfectly understood. It would be hard to say whether it arises spontaneously and voluntarily, or is the product of instinct. What does seem clear from my own observations is that bluebirds do exhibit altruism on occasion. The male bluebird's devotion to his family is in most respects fully equal to that of the female, although he will not incubate the eggs if the female should die before they are hatched. Lacking a brood patch (the bare area on the belly, richly supplied with blood vessels, which equips the female to carry out the task of incubation) the male is incapable of performing that role. But if the eggs have hatched and the nestlings are old enough not to require brooding at the time the mother bird dies, the male bluebird will usually raise the brood with the same devotion to duty that the female exhibits. If no help is available he will exert himself to raise his brood single-handedly; and he usually succeeds.

Recently a pair of bluebirds nested in a nesting box in my back yard for the first time in many years. When the second brood of nestlings was seven days old the mother bird died, possibly as a result of a massive regional insecticide spraying operation on the preceding day. Naturally we were concerned about the fate of the new brood. But the father bird never faltered in caring for his babies. Then to our surprise and immense satisfaction the two surviving young birds of the first brood, both males, soon joined their father in feeding their infant brothers and sisters. These juvenile male birds were only eight weeks old and had been capable of finding their own food for only about three weeks. Yet they contributed their full share to the support of the family, carrying food to the baby birds every few minutes from dawn to dusk for nearly a month until the younger birds had left the nest and learned to find their own food.

Again one asks what prompted these very young and immature bluebirds to undertake such a difficult and time-consuming task that is normally not expected of young birds that age. Were they "ordered" by the father bird to pitch in and help? Did they "understand" the nature and seriousness of the family emergency and volunteer their services from a sense of family loyalty? Or was it by sheer coincidence that these two young male bluebirds should be among the few of their kind that feel the urge to feed their younger siblings, and that they just happened to start doing this right at the crucial time when the family emergency arose? None of these explanations seems plausible, yet what other possible explanations can there be? We are warned against ascribing human attributes to "lower" animals, particuarly to birds which are presumed to have a low order of intelligence and to be guided only by blind instinct. Yet when we have the time and patience to·study intimately the lives of individual wild creatures we are often filled with wonder and may ask ourselves if we are really as superior to all the rest of God's creatures as our conceit has led us to believe.

Migration

By early September most bluebirds have finished their family responsibilities for the season. If they have been fortunate a pair will have produced two and in some cases three broods of young. Thus a single pair of bluebirds *may* produce as many as fifteen (and in rare instances as many as eighteen) young birds in a season. In reality, however, the hazards encountered during the nesting period and the scarcity of suitable nesting sites usually ensure that the number of surviving offspring will be much smaller.

As already noted, bluebirds maintain unusually strong family ties throughout the summer and well into the autumn season. Often in October, long after their nest has been abandoned, a family of bluebirds may be observed paying a brief return visit to the cavity or nesting box it had earlier occupied, inspecting it carefully inside and out to the accompaniment of much soft "conversation." Occasionally the birds will carry a small amount of dry grass into the cavity or box on these return visits, as though with the intention of building a new nest in the familiar site, before retiring to their winter quarters.

During most of the fall season, however, bluebird family groups tend to roam in a leisurely fashion over the countryside, searching for places where insects and possibly wild berries to their liking are to be found in greatest abundance. During the course of these wanderings family groups join with other family groups of their species to form loose flocks in preparation for the fall migration. In earlier years these flocks often contained several hundred birds. But with the great reduction in the bluebird population in more recent years they are now more likely to consist of twenty or so individuals, and often fewer.

The migration of many of our native birds is a spec-

1. Male eastern bluebird at a tree cavity

(Photo by Michael L. Smith)

2. Male eastern bluebird feeding nestlings

3. Orphaned eastern bluebirds raised by the author,
shown here at 93 days

(Photo by Lorne Scott)

4. Male mountain bluebird

(Photo by Fred Lahrman)

5. Female mountain bluebird

(Photo by Hubert W. Prescott)

6. Male western bluebird

(Photo by Hubert W. Prescott)

7. Female western bluebird

tacular affair. They may travel hundreds of miles a day, sometimes in carefully organized flocks. Many species travel by night and may fly nonstop over large bodies of water such as the Gulf of Mexico in the course of their migration. Bluebird migration, however, has none of these spectacular qualities. The southward movement of bluebirds in autumn seems to be governed more by the weather and food supply than by the calendar. As the season grows colder and the insect supply diminishes, the bluebirds withdraw from the northern parts of their breeding ranges in loose unorganized flocks and gradually move southward where food is easier to obtain. Thus, in winter they tend to congregate in the southern parts of their ranges.

To what extent migration occurs among bluebirds that breed within the bounds of the normal winter range of the species is not known. Some of these bluebirds evidently remain throughout the year near where they breed, but others appear to migrate to some extent within the winter range. Food supply is probably the governing factor. When insects are no longer available bluebirds congregate where wild berries of various kinds are plentiful.

Some bluebirds may remain in winter far north of their normal winter range in locations where there seem to be enough wild berries to last them through the winter. These birds frequently perish if heavy snow or ice covers their food supply.

The breeding range of the eastern bluebird extends from southern Canada to the Gulf of Mexico in almost all areas east of the Rockies, but in winter the bluebirds are found mainly in the southern half or two-thirds of this region. Both the western and mountain bluebirds have migratory movements in the fall to more southerly regions, or sometimes merely to lower elevations. The mountain bluebird is probably the most migratory of all bluebird species. In summer it may be found as far north as Alaska, but in winter it is usually found only south of the Canadian border, and its range then extends southward from its summer limit well into Mexico. (See Fig. 1.)

The bluebirds' fall migration may easily be explained by diminishing food supplies and the onset of cold weather in the north; but one must look for a different and less obvious explanation for the spring migration. Why should these gentle birds choose to leave the comfort and security of their winter homes in the south, where food is plentiful, and return to the rigors of the north in early March before winter has really ended, where they may perish from cold and hunger in unseasonable weather? We can only guess that they are obeying a primitive urge to produce new generations of their species in the same general area in which they and their ancestors originated. The timing of this urge may be governed at least in part by the lengthening daylight hours as winter recedes.

In earlier times when bluebirds were far more abundant than now, the spring migration probably served an imperative need to relieve overcrowding of the species before the commencement of the breeding season. Birds' food requirements are considerably greater at that time of year since there are many new mouths to be fed. To assure an adequate food supply for his family each male bluebird "stakes out" a piece of territory—the staking out is a metaphor, but the sense of territorial rights is very real—at nesting time. A male bluebird who has thus established himself will guard his territory zealously against other bluebirds which trespass in search of food.

The abundance of insects for food and the long daylight hours in the north during the warmer months plus the ample space for nesting territories probably provided the original incentives for the spring migration. A pattern was established, and it took the form of the strong instinct for the spring migration that persists now, even though the biological need for the migration may now be much less imperative than in the days of greater population pressures.

Bird migration is one of nature's great wonders. Its mysteries are gradually being unraveled, but we still have much to learn.

Further Reading

Bent, A. C. 1949. *Life Histories of North American Thrushes, Kinglets, and their Allies.* U. S. Natl. Mus. Bull. 196: 233–288.

Hartshorne, J. M., 1962. Behavior of the Eastern Bluebird at the nest. *The Living Bird* I: 131–149.

Krieg, D. C. 1971. *The Behavioral Patterns of the Eastern Bluebird.* N. Y. State Museum and Science Service, Bull. No. 415.

Pinkowski, B. C. 1975. *A Comparative Study of the Behavioral and Breeding Ecology of the Eastern Bluebird (Sialia sialis).* Ph.D. dissertation, 471 pp., published on demand by Xerox University Microfilms, P. O. Box 1346, Ann Arbor, Mich. 48106.

Thomas, R. H. 1946. A study of Eastern Bluebirds in Arkansas. *Wilson Bull.* 58: 143–183.

[3]
Causes of Population Decline

THERE IS NO DOUBT that the bluebird population of North America has declined drastically during the course of the last fifty years. The species most seriously affected by the population decline to date has been the eastern bluebird, whose range extends from the east coast to the Rocky Mountains, but all three species are now faced with mounting pressures. Unless steps are taken soon to reverse the trend, all of our bluebirds seem likely to dwindle in numbers and to retreat further to the less populated regions of the country. Although the reasons for the population decline are undoubtedly many and not all of them are fully understood, fortunately we do know some of the important factors that are involved.

Decline in Winter Food Supply

Bluebirds of all three species depend almost entirely on wild berries of various kinds for their winter food supply, except in those rather limited parts of their winter ranges (the deep south and west coastal areas) where insects may still be found in winter. The supply of these wild berries has diminished gradually but steadily over the years with the clearing of land for crop production, highways, shopping centers, and residential developments. The impact has been particularly acute throughout much of the winter range of the eastern bluebird.

Many of the trees and shrubs that in earlier years supplied a large part of the bluebirds' winter food are now stripped of their fruit in early autumn by hordes of starlings, which in recent years have become the predominant species of bird in so many parts of the country. The flowering dogwood in particular has always been a major source of winter food for berry-eating birds in the southeastern states. Now, however, starlings have found the dogwood's berries so palatable that often well before winter they have stripped the trees bare, leaving no berries for the bluebirds and other native species that depend on them for winter survival.

The American holly was also once an important source of winter food for bluebirds and other native birds. It is an especially important tree because its berries last well throughout the winter and usually are not eaten by starlings. Unfortunately, much of the wild holly has been cut away for use as Christmas decorations in recent years.

Adverse Weather

Bluebirds sometimes perish in large numbers when unusually severe weather occurs within their winter ranges. It happens especially when heavy snow or ice covers the available food. The greatest danger of all occurs when freezing rain coats the vegetation. Since birds require an almost continuous supply of food during the day to survive the night—especially in cold weather—continued cold following a heavy snow or freezing rain is likely to be fatal to bluebirds as well as other species. Statistics have shown (James [1961, 1962, 1963]) that severe winters are usually followed by reduced numbers of eastern bluebirds, and the same is undoubtedly true of the other bluebird species.

Exceptionally harsh weather in which large numbers of eastern bluebirds perished occurred throughout much of the south during the winters of 1894–95 (Bent [1949]), 1939–40, 1950–51, and 1957–58 (James [1961]). The same thing occasionally happens in the north in the early spring, after the bluebirds have returned to their nesting areas. Without doubt catastrophes of this kind have occurred at intervals throughout history. Until relatively recently, however, almost complete recovery from such losses appears to have taken place within three or four years because bluebirds are prolific species. More recently recovery seems to have been much slower, and since the latest catastrophic winter of 1957–58 the eastern bluebird population has remained pitifully low. It seems likely, therefore, that factors other than weather are contributing significantly to the population decline, and that these factors are either relatively new or have assumed much greater significance in recent years.

Insecticides

The greatly increased use and increased deadliness of modern insecticides, particularly persistent chlorinated hydrocarbons such as DDT, are believed to have seriously affected the populations of many species of birds and other wildlife. Birds may be killed by direct contact with some insecticides. In other cases death may result from their eating poisoned insects or feeding them to their nestlings. Most of the common insecticides are of the broad spectrum type, which kill not only the target species of insects but most other species as well. Thus the food supply for insectivorous birds in the treated areas may be largely destroyed in the wake of spraying that was carried out in an attempt to curtail only a particular kind of insect. Orchards which were once favorite haunts of bluebirds are now often so heavily treated with insecticides that few birds can survive in them.

Public concern over the effects of insecticides and other pesticides on the environment has fortunately risen to the point that the use of many of these chemical agents is being curtailed or prohibited. We may look forward to the day when effective biological (rather than chemical) control for specific species of insect pests will be developed and successfully applied without harmful consequences for wildlife and the natural environment; but the time has not yet come.

Destruction of Habitat

Bluebirds are cavity-nesting birds. With rare exceptions, they will nest only in some kind of small enclosure, which may be either natural or artificial. Except where nesting boxes are supplied nearly all bluebird nests are built in cavities in dead trees or wooden fence posts. Unlike woodpeckers and certain other cavity-nesting birds, bluebirds are unable to excavate their own cavities and are thus dependent on ones formed by the process of decay or as the result of excavation by woodpeckers or other birds.

With the steady expansion of civilization and the more intensive use of land for human purposes in North America in recent years, dead trees are now commonly destroyed rather than left to stand, and the dead branches of living trees are commonly removed. This trend has been greatly accelerated by the advent of the power saw, a device which makes it relatively easy to cut down branches and whole trees. At the same time, wooden fence posts are largely being supplanted by metal posts, which of course afford no nesting sites for bluebirds. And in many parts of the country small farms with a mixture of wood lots, hedgerows, orchards, and pastures that in earlier days provided good and varied habitat for wildlife have given way to huge commercial farms devoted to monoculture, from which the natural habitats of bluebirds and many other species have virtually been eliminated.

Thus the supply of natural cavities in which bluebirds can nest is steadily being reduced, and areas which formerly supported heavy bluebird populations can now often support few, if any, of these birds during the breeding season. Destruction of suitable breeding habitat is a well recognized factor in the population decline of almost all species of wildlife. It unquestionably has contributed to the present plight of the bluebirds.

Competition from Alien Birds

One of the leading causes—in most areas undoubtedly the major cause—of the decline in the bluebird population is the overwhelming competition for nesting sites between the bluebirds and the imported house sparrow (*Passer domesticus*) and starling (*Sturnus vulgaris*).

The house sparrow (also known as the English sparrow) was first successfully introduced into the United States from England in 1851 (Summers-Smith [1963]). It is actually one of the weaver finches, and not of the same family as the native sparrows of North America. Within the remarkably short period of fifty years it had overrun the entire country (except Alaska) as well as southern Canada and northern Mexico. Since the house sparrow is basically a cavity-nesting bird it competes directly with the bluebirds and other cavity-nesting birds for nesting sites. Because of its slightly smaller size it can readily enter any hole that bluebirds can enter; and because of its exceptionally aggressive nature it can usually displace the bluebird from a disputed site.

Although house sparrows have a strong preference for the same kinds of nesting sites used by bluebirds, they are remarkably adaptable and do not actually require these enclosures, as bluebirds do. If natural or artificial cavities are not available sparrows will nest in crevices or under the eaves of buildings or in vines, trees, and many other places. Hence the sparrow population is not seriously restricted by the shortage of cavities.

House sparrows do not migrate and consequently in rural environs where they are numerous they often lay claim during the winter to nearly all of the potential bluebird nesting sites and begin nesting in them before the bluebirds appear on the scene. Returning bluebirds in the spring then find they have no place to nest; and if they do succeed in eventually locating suitable unoccupied cavities or nesting boxes, they are very likely to be driven out by sparrows that subsequently take a fancy to the same sites.

Sparrows may evict bluebirds at any stage of the nesting cycle. If there are eggs in the nest the sparrows often break them and throw them out. If young bluebirds are in the nest, the sparrows may peck them to death in a characteristic fashion, always striking at the head. Afterward the sparrows will either toss the dead bluebird nestlings out of the nest or, if the corpses are too large, leave them where they lie and proceed to build their own nests on top of the dead nestlings. When one of the adult bluebirds—usually the male—attempts to intervene during such a massacre, it too is often killed and left in the nest as the sparrows build their nest over its body. It is a fairly common experience when removing a sparrow nest from a bluebird box to find a bluebird nest with a dead adult male bluebird directly underneath the sparrow nest. The bluebird almost always shows the telltale fatal peck marks over most of its head. In such cases it is obvious that the bluebird perished in a brave but futile attempt to defend his nest against a marauding house sparrow.

Starlings were first introduced into North America from Europe in 1890 (Chapman [1924]) when eighty of the birds were released in New York City's Central Park. As with the house sparrow, the alien species spread across the country with amazing rapidity. Starlings are now abundant in all states except Alaska and Hawaii and have also spread to southern Canada and northern Mexico. In a great many areas they have now become the predominant species of bird.

A half century ago Chapman [1924] foresaw all too astutely that the eastern bluebird would be seriously threatened by the introduction of the starling. Starlings nest in cavities and thus like the house sparrows they compete directly with bluebirds and other cavity-nesting birds. Although bluebirds are sometimes able to defend their nesting sites against house sparrows and thus maintain a minimal population in sparrow-infested areas, they can *never* compete successfully with starlings for the use of any cavity that the starlings can enter. So wherever starlings are numerous during the breeding season bluebirds disappear almost completely unless man intervenes in their behalf. The only exceptions occur in those very rare and diminishing areas where there are more than enough cavities to satisfy the needs of all the starlings.

Most cavity-nesting birds other than bluebirds are able to escape the ravages of the house sparrows and starlings by nesting in heavily wooded areas where neither of the imported species chooses to nest. Unfortunately bluebirds also shun the deep woods for nesting.

Thus they lack an innate means of self-preservation that is present for most other cavity nesters.

Both house sparrows and starlings like to stay close to human habitations. During their early years in North America the habitats of these birds were therefore confined largely to cities and towns and their suburbs, and it was not long afterward that the bluebirds were obliged to abandon these areas during the nesting season. Later house sparrows and then starlings gradually spread into rural areas and adapted very readily to rural life. Here again the bluebirds are being harassed and find it necessary to withdraw to more remote areas that are still relatively free from the troublesome foreigners.

Even in rural settings house sparrows maintain their strong affinity for human habitations and generally nest within half a mile or so of houses, barns, or other buildings. Starlings, on the other hand, have in recent years been penetrating deeper and deeper into wilder regions, particularly along the banks of streams, the edges of woodlands, and semi-open areas with scattered trees. Since these are the very areas to which the bluebirds have been forced to retreat, if the present trend continues it appears that starlings may in the foreseeable future occupy all of the acceptable bluebird habitat throughout North America. Starlings and house sparrows would then dominate virtually all of the natural cavities that bluebirds can use for nesting.

This extreme competition for nesting sites is an entirely unnatural situation brought about by man's folly in introducing undesirable alien species of wildlife into North America. Bluebirds are poorly equipped to cope with the situation. They can rarely defend themselves against the intruders, and seldom adapt by selecting nesting sites not sought after by the imported birds. If starlings, in particular, should manage to expand their population throughout the bluebird breeding areas—and there is every indication that they may—the bluebirds' plight is sure to worsen. Only timely intervention on man's part can now reverse the course of events originally set in motion by man's ecological shortsightedness.

Tobacco Barn Smokestacks

A curious yet quite serious hazard to bluebirds and perhaps other cavity-nesting birds in certain tobacco growing areas was recently brought to light (Finch [1972]). In part due to expressions of concern by conservationists and in part due to changing technology, the hazard now appears to have been considerably reduced, although not quite eliminated. But the story of how several million bluebirds apparently perished in only a few years after a certain form of technology came into use is worth recording, both because it probably accounts in part for the presently much-reduced state of the eastern bluebird population and because it suggests how man may quite unwittingly endanger his fellow creatures.

Beginning around 1947 pot-type oil burners came into widespread use throughout much of the south for curing tobacco on the farm where it is grown. These burners are equipped with smokestacks that extend through the roofs of the curing barns, and the tops of the smokestacks are fitted with rain caps (see Figure 8). In late winter and early spring, when the burners are not in use, bluebirds are attracted to the rain caps, the openings of which look as if they might well be entrances to suitable nesting cavities. In the course of their exploration, many of the birds slip down into the smokestack and fall to the burner below. Unable to escape back up the smokestack, the birds are trapped and die, even though the burner is unlit at that time of year.

At first thought it might seem improbable that the hazard thus posed could have had a serious impact on the bluebird population. But on the basis of responses to a questionnaire sent out to users of the tobacco-curing burners Finch estimated that during the seven years following 1947, when the burners first came into widespread use, approximately two million bluebirds died in the manner just described. From 1955 onward relatively fewer birds perished in the burners for the simple reason that few were to be found any longer in the areas in which the curing barns are located.

Finch theorized, probably correctly, that not only local bluebirds but many that had migrated from further north must have died in the curing barns. Bluebirds char-

8. Tobacco barn smokestacks with unprotected raincaps—a seriou hazard to bluebirds

(Photo by Jack R. Finch)

acteristically explore all types of holes above the ground that are large enough to admit them. They do this especially in late winter and early spring, even if they have not yet returned to their nesting areas. Thus the impact on the eastern bluebird population would not have been confined to the particular localities of the curing barns.

Acting on his findings, Finch organized a campaign to urge tobacco farmers to install bird screens in the openings of the smokestack rain caps. Made of half-inch hardware cloth, the screens are simple, inexpensive—and effective. Finch was joined by conservation groups such as the Audubon Naturalist Society and the Maryland Ornithological Society, which brought the newly discovered hazard to cavity-nesting birds to the attention of the Secretary of Agriculture. In due course the Agriculture and Interior departments directed their agents in the tobacco-growing states to encourage the use of the bird screens. By coincidence, it appears that the particular kind of tobacco-curing apparatus that had caused the hazard is gradually becoming obsolete. So there is hope that this particular threat to the bluebirds will eventually disappear.

Further Reading

Atkinson, B. 1974. Fewer bluebirds are heralding spring's return. *Smithsonian* 5 (1): 38–45.

Finch, J. R. 1972. *Disappearance of the Eastern Bluebird in Tobacco Producing Areas.* (Report distributed by the author. Address: Route 1, Bailey, N. C. 27807).

James, D. 1963. The changing seasons. *Audubon Field Notes* 17: 300–304.

Miller, W. 1970. Factors influencing the status of Eastern and Mountain Bluebirds in southwestern Manitoba. *The Blue Jay* 28: 38–46.

[4]

What Can We Do to Save the Bluebirds?

THE LOSS OF any form of wildlife is sad indeed to contemplate, for as William Beebe eloquently observed, "another heaven and another earth must pass" before a vanished form of life can be restored. But the loss of such delightful and beneficial birds as the bluebirds would be especially tragic. Could it happen though? The answer is that it need not, but unquestionably could. One has only to remember the fate of the passenger pigeon, a bird once so numerous in North America that many travellers' reports attest it literally darkened the sky in its migrations, so numerous in fact that even up to a few short years before it suddenly disappeared forever from the face of the earth it was thought incredible that it could ever be extinguished—but extinguished it was, in 1914. It is up to mankind to decide whether or not the bluebirds, like the passenger pigeon and other forms of wildlife that until only recently graced our world, should be permitted to sink gradually into oblivion.

We know at least some of the leading causes of the bluebirds' plight, and it lies within our power to act. What is needed now, before it is too late, is a nationwide effort to halt and reverse the long, gradual downward trend in the bluebird population. Although as has already been noted the western and mountain bluebirds may not yet be experiencing as serious difficulties as their eastern relative, the trend among them seems to be the same. Starlings have only recently reached the west coast, after all, but they are now undergoing a population explosion there that already seems to be having the predictable consequences for bluebirds. The mountain bluebird appears to be holding its own in the more mountainous parts of its breeding range, where environmental changes and competition from alien species of birds have been relatively slight. At lower elevations, however, the mountain bluebird too is increasingly faced with the same difficulties that the other two bluebird species face, and is suffering accordingly.

If the time for action on behalf of bluebirds is at hand, what can be done?

Nesting Sites

By far the most urgent need of the bluebirds is for nesting sites to supplement the rapidly dwindling supply of natural cavities available to them. Bluebirds will readily accept nesting boxes (bird houses, as they are commonly known) if they are located in suitable bluebird habitat and if they are designed and mounted in a manner that will afford the necessary protection. Organized efforts to help the bluebirds by providing nesting boxes have had remarkable success, often resulting in local restoration of the bluebird population to normal levels within only a few years. Detailed instructions for making simple but effective bluebird nesting boxes, for mounting them, and for selecting good locations for them, will be given in the succeeding chapters.

Winter Food

Since in winter bluebirds depend almost entirely on wild berries for food and the supply of this natural food has been greatly reduced in many areas in recent years, food supply is obviously of decisive importance in determining not only the winter ranges but ultimately the survival of all species of bluebirds.

Plantings of trees, shrubs, and vines which bear berries that last well throughout the winter will provide much-needed food for wintering bluebirds and other berry-eating birds (such as robins, waxwings, mockingbirds, etc.). To be of benefit, these plantings need not be confined to the rural areas where bluebirds are normally found during the summer months. In winter the birds frequently move closer to centers of human habitation in their search for food.

Plantings should be adapted to the regions in which they are used, of course. Consult local nurserymen or county agricultural extension agents about which species are best adapted to a particular area and about the best planting times for that area. Berry-bearing trees and shrubs are not only beneficial to birds. Most of them are also highly ornamental. A partial listing of plantings that bear good supplies of winter berries attractive to bluebirds follows:

Common name	Botanical name
Red chokeberry	Aronia arbutifolia
Spicebush	Benzoin aestivale
Bittersweet	Celastrus scandens
Hackberry	Celtis occidentalis
Flowering dogwood	Cornus florida
Small-leaved cotoneaster	Cotoneaster microphylla
Washington hawthorn	Crataegus phaenopyrum
Blackthorn	Crataegus tomentosa
Inkberry	Ilex glabra
Smooth winterberry	Ilex laevigata
American holly	Ilex opaca
Black alder	Ilex verticillata
Western red cedar	Juniperus scopulorum
Red cedar	Juniperus virginiana
Privet	Ligustrum vulgare
Amur honeysuckle	Lonicera maacki
Moonseed	Menispermum canadense
Bayberry	Myrica carolinensis
Sour gum	Nyssa sylvatica
Virginia creeper	Parthenocissus quinquefolia
Pyracantha	Pyracantha sp.
Small sumac	Rhus copallina
Smooth sumac	Rhus glabra
Staghorn sumac	Rhus typhina
Multiflora rose	Rosa multiflora
Mountain ash	Sorbus americana
Coralberry	Symphoricarpos orbiculatus
High-bush cranberry	Viburnum opulus
Black haw	Viburnum prunifolium

Special mention should be made of the American holly as a source of winter bluebird food. In early winter the berries of this lovely tree are hard and evidently unpalatable to most birds. Thus holly berries almost always remain on the tree until late winter and then soften, providing food for the birds just at the most critical time of the year. By the time holly berries are ready for consumption most other kinds of berries have been consumed or have fallen. For once, the cards are stacked in favor of the bluebirds, since for some unknown reason starlings, which often strip other trees and shrubs of their berries early in the season, rarely eat holly berries even after they have softened.

Male and female flowers of the American holly are borne on separate trees. In holly plantings, most of the trees should be female, but an occasional male tree is necessary for pollination to take place.

The multiflora rose also deserves special mention because of its rapid and vigorous growth and dependable heavy crop of berry-like fruit. Starlings will eat some of the fruit on the outer parts of these shrubs, but usually will not go into the dense, thorny interior. Bluebirds seem more assiduous in this regard. A good planting of multiflora roses will assure them an ample supply of fruit throughout the winter.

When planted as a hedge (as it often is on large estates) the multiflora rose forms a tall, dense, living fence virtually impenetrable by man or beast. It may be an undesirable planting on small plots of land, however, because of the difficulty of controlling its rapid growth and spread.

Bluebirds are not common visitors to winter feeding stations, but they can sometimes be enticed to feeders where they will eat raisins or other fruits or berries, peanut hearts (Fast [1955]) or chopped unsalted peanuts, suet, or sometimes even a little cracked corn. Bluebirds are not seed eaters, so they find very little they can eat in the seed mixtures commonly used for feeding wild birds. When the berries they depend upon for their winter sustenance are covered with snow or ice, every effort should be made to provide food for bluebirds and any other berry-eating birds that may be in the vicinity.

Protection from Cold

Bluebirds and other birds that winter in the United States or Canada instead of flying to the tropics are often forced to endure considerable hardship. Cold weather alone is usually tolerated well enough, provided that the food supply is adequate and that the birds can find a sheltered place to sleep at night. Birds generate an impressive amount of body heat and their feathers provide superb insulation against external cold.

Bluebirds are not one of our hardiest birds, and as has already been noted, during certain severe winters in the south untold thousands of them have perished from the combined effects of cold and insufficient food. When birds are forced to go to roost hungry their fires of life burn low; and if the weather is severe many will perish. These are the times when a protected place to roost at night may spell the difference between life and death.

Cavity-nesting birds and occasionally other kinds of birds as well that winter in cold climates often use natural cavities in trees, old woodpecker holes, and nesting boxes for night roosting. Sometimes they take refuge in such places only during the severest weather; at other times, they will sleep in them regularly throughout the winter. A number of birds may huddle together in a single cavity or nesting box for the night (Frazier and Nolan [1959]), taking advantage of the additional warmth produced by their numbers. Thus nesting boxes that are left in place during the winter may serve a useful purpose.

Strictly speaking, however, nesting boxes are not ideal for overnight roosting in winter. They are too small to accommodate many birds. Being designed for summer habitation, they allow for much more ventilation than is desirable on a cold night. Moreover, the positioning of the entrance hole near the top of a nesting box allows valuable warmth from the birds' bodies to escape upward.

A good roosting box is large enough to accommodate a considerable number of birds. For bluebirds and other small birds, one with inside floor dimensions of 10" x 10" and a depth of 18" to 24" is good. The entrance hole should be at or near the floor level. If the entrance is about 2" in diameter it will admit most of the smaller birds. If starlings take an interest in the box, however, the entrance should be reduced to 1½", otherwise starlings will soon be the only birds to use it. A perch below the opening is helpful. Without one, some birds might have difficulty entering a box that has its entrance at floor level. (Obviously if a perch is to be included the entranceway must be slightly above floor level.) No openings should be made higher up in the box; but a small opening for drainage should be made near each corner of the floor.

Several horizontal perches (which can be made of

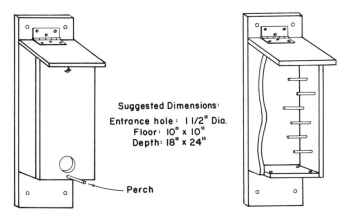

Suggested Dimensions:
Entrance hole : 1 1/2" Dia.
Floor : 10" x 10"
Depth : 18" x 24"

— Perch

9. Plans for a winter roosting box

This winter roosting box should be mounted on a pole or post at least six feet above the ground and should be protected from predators. It may be used by bluebirds, chickadees, titmice, nuthatches, wrens, and the smaller woodpeckers.

$\frac{1}{2}''$ dowels) should be positioned at various levels within the box—staggered, rather than placed directly above one another, for sanitary reasons. The top, bottom, or one side of the box should be hinged or otherwise made to open easily for cleaning.

One or more of the inside surfaces of the roosting box, including the front, should be roughened for the benefit of woodpeckers, should any decide to use the box. Woodpeckers prefer to sleep while clinging to a perpendicular surface like the trunk of a tree.

Figure 9 shows a good winter roosting box. The birds that are most likely to make use of it are bluebirds, chickadees, titmice, nuthatches, and woodpeckers. If the entrance hole is made 3″ rather than 2″ in diameter as suggested above, flickers or screech owls may use the box.

Roosting boxes are preferably mounted on smooth metal posts, and the posts should be kept greased if there are predators in the vicinity that might try to scale them. It is also a good idea to mount the boxes in protected spots and to face them southward for greatest warmth.

As many as a dozen bluebirds have been known to roost regularly during winter in a single box of the kind shown here.

Further Reading

Gannon, R. 1962. To bring back the bluebird. *Reader's Digest,* March 1962: 231–236.

Musselman, T. E. 1934. Help the bluebirds. *Bird-Lore* 36: 9–13.

[5]

Bluebird
Nesting Boxes
(Bird Houses)

THE ONLY KNOWN practical way that we can help the bluebirds in the desperate situation that they now face at nesting time is to supply them with sufficient numbers of properly made starling-proof nesting boxes (bird houses) and to take whatever steps may be necessary to keep house sparrows from using them.

Nesting boxes for bluebirds have been used with varying degrees of success for many years, and numerous conflicting opinions have arisen in regard to the proper construction of these boxes. Fortunately bluebirds are not at all particular and seem to be quite willing to use almost any kind of box that they can enter, provided it is in the right kind of location and is not already occupied. It is important, however, to adhere to certain basic requirements in order to prevent, as far as possible, competing species from occupying the boxes, and to offer the greatest possible protection to the bluebirds from their enemies and from adverse weather.

This chapter will discuss the principles of proper bluebird nesting box design and present detailed plans and instructions for making two types of simple wooden nesting boxes, both of which have been thoroughly tested and found to be highly successful in practical use. Instructions are also given for making "no-cost" bluebird houses from discarded plastic jugs. These show promise for helping to solve the house sparrow problem, but until they can be more extensively tested they are recommended only for experimental use.

Material

Wood is both the most satisfactory and the most commonly used material for the construction of nesting boxes. Almost any kind of wood will do—including scrap lumber, which can sometimes be obtained at little or no cost. Pine is easy to work with and the relatively inexpensive Number 3 grade (also known as "construction grade") is usually adequate. "Cedar" (juniper), cypress, and redwood are more weather-resistant, but also more expensive. (Cedar boards intended for fencing but suitable for nesting boxes may often be obtained at a reasonable price, however.) Avoid lumber that is warped or split. Exterior grade plywood is excellent for nesting boxes. It weathers well and will not warp. Plywood that is not designated for exterior use should never be used, since it will deteriorate rapidly when exposed to the weather.

Lumber for nesting boxes should be at least ¾" thick to provide adequate insulation against heat on hot sunny days. The insulation is all to the good when abnormally cold weather strikes during the nesting season as well. The nails used for nesting boxes should either be galvanized or made of aluminum. Nails with roughened shanks (designed to hold tightly) are superior to smooth nails, although slightly more expensive. Galvanized siding nails of either 12½ or 14 gauge, 1¾″ long, are excellent, and are commonly available. Screws may be used instead of nails but the added expense is hardly justified.

Bluebird nesting boxes should never be made of metal or translucent plastic unless steps are taken to prevent them from overheating when exposed to the sun's rays.

ENTRANCE TO THE NESTING BOX

The size of the entrance hole is by far the most critical dimension of the bluebird nesting box. The diameter of the hole should not be greater than 1½″ nor smaller than 1⁷⁄₁₆″. All species of bluebirds can readily enter any hole within this very limited range, but starlings are effectively excluded. Entrance holes 1⅝″ and even as large as 1¾″ in diameter have sometimes been recommended; but since they will admit starlings entrance holes that large should never be used in areas where starlings are present. (See Zeleny [1969].)

Some commercial bluebird nesting boxes come with openings only 1⅜″ in diameter. Most eastern bluebirds seem able to enter boxes with entrance holes that small without too much trouble, although the fit is somewhat tight. Some of the birds manage to enter only with difficulty, and a few seem unable—or unwilling—to enter at all. Since a 1⅜″ opening is not small enough to keep out house sparrows and since it seems to be slightly too small to suit some bluebirds, it is not recommended.

DEPTH OF THE BOX

The depth of the nesting box is the distance from the bottom of the entrance hole on the inside of the box to the floor of the box. (The distance from the entrance hole to the top of the box is not of importance.)

Although starlings cannot actually enter a nesting box with an opening $1\frac{1}{2}''$ in diameter, they will certainly try. If bluebirds are nesting in the box, the starlings will often disrupt the nest by reaching through the opening. If they can reach in far enough they may break the eggs or kill the nestlings. It has sometimes been reported that starlings have even managed to kill female bluebirds while they were engaged in incubating their eggs or brooding their nestlings. If the depth of the box (measured from the bottom of the entrance hole to the floor) is appreciably less than six inches, starlings often succeed in reaching the nest within, with disastrous results for the bluebirds. However, if the depth is six inches or more and the front of the box is at least $\frac{3}{4}''$ thick, starlings cannot actually get at the nest unless it has been built up to a much higher than normal level in the box. The top of a bluebird's nest is usually less than four inches from the floor of a nesting box, but occasionally it may be as much as six inches or even more.

Some instructions for making bluebird nesting boxes provide for a depth of considerably less than six inches. Many commercially made boxes are also rather shallow. Such boxes are readily enough accepted by the bluebirds, but expose the birds to danger wherever starlings are present.

Nesting box depths of more than six inches sometimes help to reduce the danger of predation by raccoons and certain other animals that prey on bluebirds (see Chapter 9).

It is sometimes recommended that the inside of the front board of the nesting box be roughened or even fitted with a series of small cleats to give the young birds a foothold when they scramble up to leave the nest. Careful studies, however, have shown that young bluebirds about to be fledged can easily make their way up and out of nesting boxes that are as much as ten inches deep, even though the inside of the box is perfectly smooth. It is possible, though, that young tree swallows or violet-green swallows may have some difficulty getting out of deep nesting boxes. Therefore in those areas where these swallows are likely to use the bluebird nesting boxes, it may be a wise precaution to roughen the inside of the front board or provide it with cleats if the depth of the box is more than six inches. The cleats should be about ⅛ " thick and ¼ " wide and spaced about an inch apart horizontally on the inside of the front board between the floor and the entrance hole. A piece of ½ " hardware cloth attached to the same area would serve the same purpose.

There are two schools of thought regarding the best inside floor dimensions for bluebird nesting boxes. One school recommends a 5 " x 5 " floor (giving a total area of 25 square inches). Other bluebird conservationists believe that a 4 " x 4 " floor (16 square inches) is preferable. Most published instructions specify the larger floor. These larger boxes are acceptable to all three species of bluebirds and provide ample room for the largest broods. The popularity of the smaller boxes derives in part from their closer resemblance to the size of the nesting cavities hewn out of dead trees by downy woodpeckers. Since these are among the natural cavities most commonly used by bluebirds (after the woodpeckers have finished using them) there is an obvious case for constructing nesting boxes on a similar scale. Nesting boxes with the smaller floors are lighter and thus easier to mount, are more economical to make, and provide plenty of room for the bluebirds under most circumstances. An additional advantage is that to some extent the smaller boxes discourage house sparrows from moving in. House sparrows like to build bulky nests, and where there is a choice they are likely to choose larger boxes to nest in. Where house sparrows are numerous, even a small advantage to be gained for the bluebirds should not be overlooked.

Nesting boxes with floors as small as $3\frac{1}{2}$" x $3\frac{1}{2}$" ($12\frac{1}{4}$ square inches) or even 3" x 3" (a mere 9 square inches) may be used by bluebirds and are even less attractive to house sparrows, but are not recommended for general use because of the crowded conditions they create for the larger broods.

On balance, I recommend the 4" x 4" floor, except where house sparrows are not a problem and perhaps within the breeding ranges of the western and mountain bluebirds. For the latter two species, whose broods tend to be slightly larger than those of the eastern bluebird, the 5″ x 5″ floor may have some advantage. The mountain bluebird is also a slightly larger bird than either of the other species, and for this reason would benefit somewhat from the more spacious nesting box.

PROVISION FOR OPENING THE BOX

Many nesting boxes, including some of the commercially made ones, can be opened only by prying off the top or one side, or by the removal of several nails or screws. This is a serious drawback. The box should be easy to open both for observation and for removal of sparrows' nests and old nests of bluebirds and other birds that are no longer being used. On the other hand, a box that can be opened too easily invites vandalism and increases the chance that curious passers-by will disturb the nesting birds. A satisfactory compromise is a box whose top or side can be opened by the removal of a single screw or nut. If the box is on private property where vandalism is not likely to be a problem, it may be more convenient to make it so that it can be opened by unfastening a hook or removing a wing nut without the aid of a tool.

Boxes that are going to be monitored frequently should allow access from above rather than from the side, since an approach from above is least likely to cause disturbance to the occupants. Side-opening or front-opening boxes have the advantage of being somewhat easier to clean when the time comes to remove old nests. They also make it easier to take good photographs of the nests, eggs, and nestlings. A decided disadvantage of the front- or side-opening type of box, however, is that if it is opened when it contains nestlings more than about twelve days old, the young birds may become agitated to the point of taking flight prematurely. Even if they are captured and returned to the nest immediately, they will usually leave it again as soon as possible, and nestlings that leave the nest prematurely have greatly reduced prospects for survival.

PERCHES

Bluebirds have no need for perches and none should be attached to their nesting boxes, since house sparrows find them quite useful in maintaining possession of boxes they have once managed to occupy.

PROTECTION FROM RAIN

To minimize the chance that rain will be blown into the box, the roof of the nesting box should overhang the entrance hole and all ventilation holes. For the same reason it is desirable that the roof slope toward the front of the box.

VENTILATION AND DRAINAGE

Small openings for ventilation should be provided close to the top of the nesting box, where they will be protected from rain by the overhanging roof. The vents will help to prevent overheating of the box on hot days.

Openings for drainage should also be provided in the floor, since rain is sometimes blown in through the entrance hole. Drainage holes are best made by cutting away about ⅜" from each corner of the bottom board.

PAINTING THE NESTING BOX

Painting or staining the nesting box is not really necessary, but it may improve its appearance and will unquestionably add years to its life, especially if the box is built of pine. If the box is to be painted, modern exterior latex paints are excellent and are easy to apply. Aluminum paint is also satisfactory. Exterior oil-based paints may also be used, of course; but if an oil paint is chosen take care to select one that contains no lead, to avoid any possibility of harm to the birds through lead poisoning.

In general, it is a good idea to select a light-colored rather than a dark-colored paint or stain, since darker colors absorb more heat and may endanger the eggs or nestlings on hot summer days as well as make the nesting box less comfortable for the adult bluebirds. Temperatures in dark-colored nesting boxes may be as much as 12° F. higher than in light-colored boxes of the same design and construction (Zeleny [1968]). White is the best color from the standpoint of temperature control, but white boxes are conspicuous, and thus perhaps more often subject to vandalism. Light shades of green, gray, or tan tend to blend in well with natural surroundings and are the most satisfactory colors for nesting boxes.

The top board generally deteriorates more quickly than the other parts of the nesting box. If left unpainted it may warp, causing small cracks that will accelerate its deterioration. For this reason it is a good practice to paint the top board of the nesting box with two coats of exterior latex or aluminum paint on both sides and all edges even if the rest of the box is left unpainted. If the top board is made of a good grade of exterior plywood or hardboard, however, it will not warp and need not necessarily be painted. The interior of the box (except for the top board) and the exposed rim of the entrance hole should not be painted. Although chemical wood preservatives add to the life of a nesting box, some of them are highly toxic. I advise against using them in order to avoid any risk of harming the occupants of the box. If preservatives are used, they should be applied only to the outside of the box. They should not be applied to the rim of the entrance hole, where the birds would come into direct contact with them.

PLANS FOR WOODEN BLUEBIRD NESTING BOXES

Detailed plans for a top-opening bluebird nesting box with a floor measuring 4″ x 4″ (inside dimensions) are given in Fig. 10. Figure 11 gives plans for a side-opening box with a 5″ x 5″ floor. Either type may be constructed in either size with the appropriate changes in the dimensions of the component parts.*

Many people like to add architectural embellishments to their bluebird boxes, which is fine as long as the basic requirements described in this chapter are adhered to. Gabled bird houses, for example, are often quite attractive. It hardly needs to be said that the embellishments

---

* Bluebird nesting boxes of the type shown in Figure 10 are available from the Audubon Naturalist Society, 8940 Jones Mill Road, Washington, D.C. 20015.

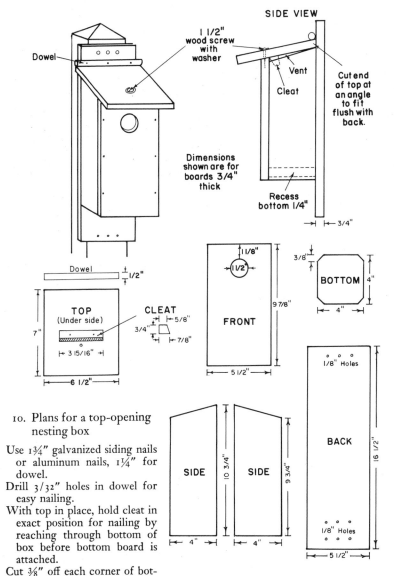

SIDE VIEW

Dowel

1 1/2" wood screw with washer

Vent

Cleat

Cut end of top at an angle to fit flush with back.

Dimensions shown are for boards 3/4" thick

Recess bottom 1/4"

3/4"

Dowel

1/2"

TOP
(Under side)

7"

3 15/16"

6 1/2"

CLEAT

5/8"

3/4"

7/8"

FRONT

1 1/8"

1/2"

9 7/8"

5 1/2"

BOTTOM

3/8"

4"

4"

1/8" Holes

BACK

16 1/2"

1/8" Holes

5 1/2"

SIDE

10 3/4"

4"

SIDE

9 3/4"

4"

10. Plans for a top-opening nesting box

Use 1¾" galvanized siding nails or aluminum nails, 1¼" for dowel.

Drill 3/32" holes in dowel for easy nailing.

With top in place, hold cleat in exact position for nailing by reaching through bottom of box before bottom board is attached.

Cut ⅜" off each corner of bottom board as shown.

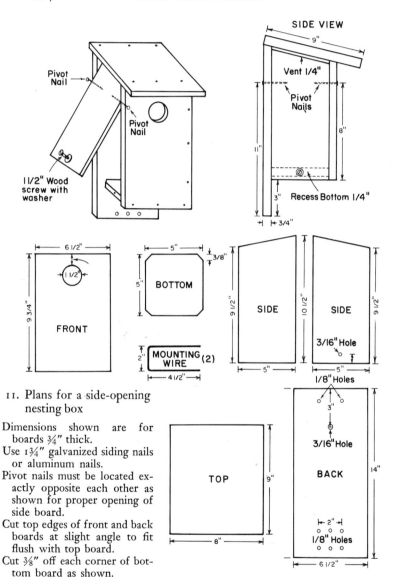

11. Plans for a side-opening
    nesting box

Dimensions shown are for
    boards ¾" thick.
Use 1¾" galvanized siding nails
    or aluminum nails.
Pivot nails must be located ex-
    actly opposite each other as
    shown for proper opening of
    side board.
Cut top edges of front and back
    boards at slight angle to fit
    flush with top board.
Cut ⅜" off each corner of bot-
    tom board as shown.
Insert bottom board so that the
    grain of the wood runs from
    front to rear of box.

are a matter of indifference to the bluebirds. They are satisfied with the simplest design tailored to their needs.

SOME NOTES ON CONSTRUCTION

Wooden nesting boxes may be made of either rough or planed lumber, but the latter is usually used because it is more readily available. It should be remembered that in the case of planed lumber the actual widths of the boards are from ½″ to ¾″ less than the nominal or advertised widths. (Thus a so-called 12″ board actually measures between 11¼″ and 11½″ in width, a '10″ board' is between 9¼″ and 9½″ wide, etc.) The proper actual widths of the boards (except the top board) specified for the nesting box with the 4″ x 4″ floor are 4″ and 5½″ (see Fig. 10). These measurements should be considered approximate, and may be arrived at readily without any waste by ripping—that is, cutting lengthwise, along the grain of the wood—10‴ lumber, which as already stated is really slightly less than 10″ in width, into the desired pieces roughly 4″ and 5½″ wide. Similarly, for the nesting box with the larger (5″ x 5″) floor area (see Fig. 11), all pieces except the top board may be fashioned by ripping so-called 12″ lumber into the required 5″ and 6½″ approximate widths.

It is worth taking a little extra care in fitting the top to the top-opening nesting box shown in Figure 10. The proper positioning of the cleat on the underside of the top board is especially important. It should be taken care of before the top is screwed in place and before the bottom board is attached to the box. The top is held in place with the left hand and the cleat is held against the insides of the front and top boards with the right hand (which should be passed through the open bottom of the box). The top board is then carefully pushed out with the right hand and the cleat grasped and held in position with the thumb of the left hand. The position of the cleat on the top board is then marked with a pencil. Before the cleat is nailed to the top board it should be moved 1/16″ toward the rear of the board to allow for expansion (which may occur in humid weather or when latex paint is applied). Note that the length of the cleat is 1/16″ less than the inside width of the box. This is also to allow for expansion and to prevent binding.

The dowel which holds the rear of the top board in place should be nailed securely (with nails at least 1¼″ long—if longer nails are used they may be bent over against the back of the box), otherwise it is likely to loosen and eventually to fall off. The nailing may be done more easily if small holes are first drilled at the points where the nails pass through the dowel. If desired, a simple tapered cleat (similar to the one used on the inside of the top board) may be used in place of the dowel to hold the rear of the top board in place. If a cleat is used, the nails should be at least 1½″ long.

With the top and dowel (or cleat) in place, a 3/16″ hole should be drilled through the top, midway between the two sides, and directly above the middle of the front board (see Fig. 10, side view). At the point where the drill strikes the top edge of the front board a starter hole no larger than 3/32″ in diameter may be drilled downward into the front board to facilitate insertion of the screw holding the top board in place. A 1½″ Number 10 round-headed wood screw, preferably of brass so that it will not rust, is recommended for fastening the top to the front board. It is a good idea to use a $\frac{1}{2}''$ washer as well; and a little grease applied to the threads makes it easier to insert and remove the screw when the box is opened for inspection.

If the box is situated where it is unlikely to be tampered with, an eye screw of the same length may be substituted for the round-headed screw, enabling the box to be opened and shut easily without the use of a screwdriver.

The screw hole in the top of the front edge of a box that has been opened many times will eventually become worn. When that happens a small plug fashioned from softwood may be driven tightly into the hole, and the screw then inserted into the plug. Or the wearing of the screw hole may be avoided at the outset by the use of a $\frac{1}{4}''$ diameter, $1''$ long screw anchor (a standard hardware store item). If an anchor is going to be used, first drill a hole of the same diameter ($\frac{1}{4}''$) downward through the top edge of the front board in lieu of a starter hole for the screw. Then spread a small amount of glue on the anchor and drive it completely into the hole. If by any chance the anchor should protrude into the entrance hole, the protruding part should be filed off. A $1\frac{1}{4}''$ screw to hold the top of the box in place is adequate when an anchor is employed.

Another way of attaching the top for a top-opening box is by means of a hinge. If a hinged top is planned, the dowel, the cleat on the back board, and the one on the inside of the top board are unnecessary. Select a brass hinge that will not rust and bind. It should be at least 2″ wide and should be attached with ¾″ wood screws. With the top held in place the hinge is screwed to the top board and to the front of the back board. The top may then be secured in the closed position by means of a single screw in the manner described above, or by a hook and eye on one side of the box.

No-Cost Plastic Nesting Boxes

Plastic containers of various kinds that are most often discarded after use have occasionally been used with some degree of success to make bird houses. These are very easy to make and are virtually cost-free. Gallon-size plastic jugs of the type commonly used for laundry bleaches and other liquids are most suitable for conversion to bluebird houses, although even half-gallon plastic or waxed cardboard milk cartons have been used successfully (Woodward [1973]). Bluebirds will often accept these jug-type houses for nesting if nothing better is available. Since these plastic jugs are discarded by the millions they can readily be obtained at no cost.

The most serious objection to bird houses made from plastic jugs is that they afford too little insulation from the sun's heat. The sun's rays easily penetrate the thin translucent plastic and overheat the jugs to the point that they may be death-traps for the embryonic bluebirds and young nestlings within. Fortunately, the problem of overheating can be eliminated by painting the exterior of the jug with two or more coats of either aluminum paint or a light-colored exterior latex paint. A jug-type bird house thus treated will remain cool enough for the birds' comfort and well-being except in extreme conditions. It is essential that at least two coats of paint be applied, more if necessary, to make the container opaque.

To make a bluebird house out of a gallon-size plastic jug first be sure that the inside is completely clean. Using a small, sharp knife, or a power drill equipped with a hole saw, cut a hole $1\frac{1}{2}''$ in diameter in the side of the jug opposite the handle. The bottom of the hole should be six inches above the bottom of the jug. If any sharp or jagged edges remain around the rim of the entrance, they should be smoothed out, and the bottom edge of the hole in particular should be slightly rounded, to prevent any possible injury to the birds' feet. A small file or a piece of fine sandpaper may be used for smoothing the entrance hole.

Four drainage holes about $\frac{3}{8}''$ in diameter should be made near the outer edge of the bottom. A similar hole for ventilation should be cut through the underside of the handle at the point where it joins the top of the jug (the point at which rain is least likely to be blown in). Two more small holes (about $\frac{3}{16}''$ in diameter) about $1\frac{3}{4}''$ apart should be made an inch from the bottom of the jug directly below the handle. A piece of Number 14 galvanized wire is then passed through these small holes to attach the jug to a post. A second wire is passed through the handle and around the post. Both wires should be tightened securely, the bottom one first, by twisting the ends together with a pair of pliers.

If a sparrow's nest should be discovered in one of the converted jugs, it can be removed with the aid of a piece of stiff wire about 18 inches long, bent into a hook at one end. The wire can be inserted through the entrance hole or through the top of the jug after removal of the cap. The jug may then be cleaned more thoroughly by hosing it out if necessary. Old bluebird nests should similarly be cleared out to make room for new ones.

Detailed plans for a plastic jug bluebird house are shown in Figure 12. Figure 13 shows one of the jug-type houses mounted on a fence post.

The contents of a nest in this type of bird house can usually be observed by peering through the entrance hole. On overcast days a little light from a flashlight beamed through the top is helpful—but don't forget to replace the cap on the top of the jug before moving on to monitor the next nesting box!

Plastic jug-type bird houses are still relatively new and they have to be studied more carefully before it can be said that they are entirely suitable. Preliminary observations suggest that when given a choice bluebirds will usually select either a natural cavity or a wooden nesting box in preference to the jug-type house, but that in the absence of choice they often take up residence in the converted jugs. There is also some rather good evidence that house sparrows may be inclined to shun the plastic jug bird houses. If this should prove to be true, it would obviously be a tremendous boon to bluebird conservation in areas densely populated by house sparrows. In any case, it is plain that the great simplicity with which the jug-type bird houses can be constructed and the fact that they are virtually cost-free should stimulate

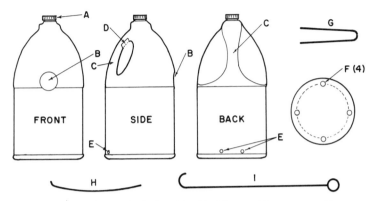

12. Plans for a plastic jug bluebird house (from one-gallon jug)

A. Cap
B. Entrance hole, 1½" diameter
C. Jug handle
D. Ventilation opening made by cutting out small section from underside of handle.
E. Mounting holes (2), 3/16" diameter
F. Drainage holes (4), ⅜" diameter
G. Upper mounting wire. Fits around jug handle and mounting post.

H. Lower mounting wire. Insert slightly hooked end (left end of wire in figure) into one mounting hole (E), then out of the other. Wind wire around post and twist ends together securely.
I. Wire for pulling out sparrows' nests and old bluebird nests. Length: 14".

Paint outside of house with at least two coats of light colored exterior latex or aluminum paint to prevent overheating.

further investigation. If subsequent studies bear out the initial promise raised by the new type of bird houses, their widespread use may make possible the establishment of extensive new bluebird trails where none would otherwise exist.

Further Reading

U.S. Department of the Interior. 1969 (rev.). *Homes for Birds*. Fish and Wildlife Serv., Conservation Bull. 14.

13. Plastic jug nesting box

[6]
Where and How to Mount the Nesting Boxes

THE SELECTION of good locations for mounting bluebird nesting boxes is actually more important than the design of the box. Too often well-meaning individuals and groups lavish care and money on the production of excellent bluebird boxes only to set them out where there is little or no prospect that bluebirds will ever use them. This chapter will describe the kinds of habitat that are most attractive to bluebirds during the nesting season and will tell how the nesting boxes should be set out for best results.

Although it was not always so, bluebirds now rarely nest within cities, large towns, or even in most suburban areas—except perhaps at their outer fringes. They seem to have learned that in these areas the competition from house sparrows and starlings is likely to be overwhelming. To be of real benefit, then, bluebird nesting boxes should be placed in far-outlying suburbs, small towns and villages, or best of all in strictly rural areas.

It should also be remembered that bluebirds seldom

nest in heavily wooded areas except along the edges of the woods and in clearings. Their preference for nesting in open areas is one reason bluebirds have such serious trouble with house sparrows and starlings. Most other cavity-nesting birds will retreat to the deep woods to build their nests if necessary to escape the ravages of the sparrows and starlings, which usually shun deep woods.

Bluebirds prefer reasonably open areas with scattered trees, especially if the trees have a few low dead branches that the birds can use for perches from which to scan the ground for insects. Open fields are satisfactory as long as there are fences or wires nearby on which the birds may perch. Pastures, open waste lands, large lawns, country cemeteries, and golf courses make good bluebird nesting locations. Abandoned orchards where no insecticides are used are favorite bluebird haunts.

Bluebirds characteristically select areas where the ground is not heavily covered with vegetation or where the grass or other vegetation is kept short by cutting or grazing. This is because bluebirds obtain most of their food from the ground which they scan for insects from overhead perches. Obviously any heavy ground cover interferes seriously with this method of feeding. Areas where the soil is of low fertility are often favored by bluebirds because these areas support only sparse vegetation. Figure 14 shows a typical bluebird habitat.

Nesting boxes should never be mounted where insecticides or herbicides are used extensively. Many of these chemicals will destroy much of the birds' food supply or may even kill the birds by poisoning them.

14. Typical bluebird habitat

Territorial Rights

During the nesting season each male bluebird stakes out a rather well defined territory for his and his mate's exclusive use. Other species of birds are generally tolerated within this territory, but any other bluebird that dares to enter is quickly driven out. Because of this insistence on territorial prerogatives, bluebirds usually will not nest closer than about a hundred yards from other bluebirds. Not much is gained, therefore, in placing the nesting boxes closer to one another than that—unless it is desired to provide nesting sites for other desirable species of cavity-nesting birds such as tree swallows, chickadees, and titmice (see Chapter 10). There is no actual harm done by situating the boxes closer than one hundred yards apart.

Height of the Box above the Ground

Bluebirds will accept nesting boxes mounted at almost any height from one to fifteen feet or even more above the ground. Very low mounting naturally increases the danger of predation. High mounting increases the chance that house sparrows will cause trouble. It also makes the boxes inaccessible for observation and cleaning unless you are prepared to carry a long ladder with you. In general, the best height for bluebird boxes is from three to five feet above the ground (as measured to the bottom of the box). At that height it is easy to observe the birds periodically during the nesting season and easy to clean the boxes whenever necessary. Since house sparrows prefer higher nesting sites, the relatively low mounting height suggested here also discourages them to some extent from taking over the bluebird boxes.

Interference with the Nesting Boxes

Parks, campgrounds, and other public places with scattered trees often appear to be ideal locations for bluebird nesting boxes—and would be, if the risk of vandalism as well as of innocent interference with the birds by careless passers-by could be reduced. Wherever there is a fair amount of foot traffic, it is a good idea to mount the boxes ten feet or so from the ground. They should also be kept at a distance from playgrounds, baseball diamonds, picnic areas, etc.

Other Considerations

When young bluebirds first leave the nest, ordinarily at the age of between fifteen and twenty days, they instinctively fly directly to something—usually a tree—that will afford them a perch above the ground where they will be reasonably safe from predators in their first crucial hours out of the nest. It is good to face the nesting box toward a tree with low branches, a large shrub, or a fence that is within fifty feet or so. If there are good perches in several directions, face the box away from the direction of the prevailing winds, if possible, to reduce the chance that rain will be driven in through the entrance hole.

Nesting boxes are much less likely to be occupied by house sparrows if they are kept at a good distance from buildings and from places where animals, poultry, or wild birds are fed. If sparrows are not a problem locally, however, it is quite possible to induce bluebirds to take up residence within twenty feet or so of one's house.

House wrens (another serious competitor for bluebird nesting sites—see Chapter 10) are less likely to interfere with the bluebirds if the nesting boxes are placed well away from shrubbery and underbrush.

Where climbing predators are a problem the nesting boxes should be mounted on posts with sheet metal guards or other means of protection (see Chapter 9) rather than on trees. Otherwise they may be attached to the trunks of isolated trees but never among the branches.

Fence posts are convenient locations for nesting boxes if there is not much local danger of predation. The boxes should be placed on the side of the fence away from any livestock to prevent damage by the animals. Any vines or other vegetation that may be growing on or near the fence should be trimmed away from the boxes.

Utility poles make excellent mounts for bluebird boxes. Permission should be sought beforehand, however. If the boxes are mounted on the north or northeast side of the poles they will be protected from the most intense heat of the sun.

Joseph Huber of Heath, Ohio, conceived the novel idea of attaching bluebird nesting boxes to rural mailbox posts directly underneath the mailboxes. He found that the birds readily accepted this arrangement and seemed not to be appreciably disturbed by the daily delivery and collection of the mail. Readers who wish to adopt Mr. Huber's method should build boxes of the side-opening type similar to the one shown in Fig. 11, except that the top of the box should be flat rather than sloping. If the mailbox is near a well travelled road, the nesting box should be faced away from the road.

Mounting the Boxes

The nesting boxes shown in Figures 10 and 11 may be attached to the tops or sides of wooden posts by means of screws or nails through the holes in the back boards. Or they may be bolted or wired to the tops or sides of

15. Nesting box mounted on top of a metal post. (The box shown is the extra-deep kind designed to give added protection from raccoons.)

16. Nesting box mounted on the side of a metal fencepost

17. Nesting box hung on a utility pole with wire

18. Nesting box mounted on galvanized pipe with pipe flange

(Photo by Joseph F. Huber)

19. Nesting box mounted on a mailbox post.

metal posts. When metal fence posts are used, U-shaped pieces of Number 14 galvanized wire like the one shown in Figure 11 can easily be slipped through the small holes in the back boards and twisted tightly around the fence posts for a simple and secure mounting.

One of the neatest and most satisfactory ways to mount a nesting box is to attach a six or seven foot length of ½" or ⅜" (inside diameter) galvanized water pipe, threaded at one end, to the bottom of the box by means of a pipe flange (obtainable at hardware stores). The un-threaded end of the pipe is inserted about two feet into the ground. A ground auger is handy for this installation. For more permanent installation the pipe may be set in concrete. If the exposed portion of the pipe is then kept heavily coated with soft automobile grease during the nesting season, most climbing predators will be kept away. (For a fuller discussion of predator control, see Chapter 9.)

Figures 15–19 show various methods for mounting the nesting boxes.

Further Reading

Kibler, L. F. 1969. The establishment and maintenance of a blue-bird nest-box project. A review and commentary. *Bird-Banding* 40: 114–129.

[7]
Monitoring the Nesting Boxes

SINCE WILD BIRDS are usually quite able to look after their own affairs, why not just set out nesting boxes in suitable bluebird habitat and let nature take its course? At first thought this seems reasonable. Most wildlife, one suspects, is better off without attention from mankind. Why not bluebirds?

The case of the bluebirds is somewhat special because man has upset the balance of nature for them not just by destroying their natural nesting sites but by introducing alien species of birds whose spread and multiplication have left the bluebirds at a great disadvantage. No single cause but rather a combination of causes has reduced the bluebird population to its present low state. For successful rehabilitation of the bluebirds to take place now, it is essential not only to provide them with nesting sites but to do whatever else is needed to protect the birds from their enemies, both native and imported, during the nesting season. By monitoring the nesting boxes frequently and taking whatever steps seem necessary to safeguard the nests, it is usually possible to increase considerably the number of young birds successfully raised. When there are only one or two nesting boxes to monitor and they are near one's home, daily monitoring poses no difficulties. In the case of an extensive bluebird trail, daily inspection may be out of the question. If possible, the boxes should be checked at least once a week during the nesting season. Frequent monitoring is especially important wherever house sparrows are a problem.

Won't the opening of a nesting box for inspection frighten the birds within into deserting their nest? The answer is that it will not, if the box has been designed for easy monitoring and the observer uses common sense in the course of his inspection. Top-opening boxes produce the least interference with the nesting birds, of course, but even the side-opening boxes can safely be opened for inspection if it is done with care. As previously noted, however, it is best not to open a side-opening box after the nestlings are twelve days old, lest they might be stimulated to leave the nest prematurely. Unless there are definite signs of trouble requiring action on the part of the person inspecting the box, a quick look should suffice. Then the box should be closed promptly, and the inspector should withdraw from the vicinity of the box. Ordinarily there should be no need to open a nesting box more than once a day while the birds are nesting in it.

Watching the progress of a bluebird family in this way can be a source of great pleasure and satisfaction, and children who are brought along on an inspection tour always find it fascinating to see at first hand one of nature's wonders. It hardly needs saying, however, that young children should be carefully supervised in their examination of nesting birds of any kind. The pages that follow describe some of the things to look for in the course of making the rounds of bluebird nesting boxes to inspect them.

The Season's Initial Monitoring

Boxes that have been left out all winter should be inspected before the beginning of the nesting season. Early February is the time to do it in the south; in the north, early March. Old nesting material and other debris that may have found its way into the boxes should be removed. A check should be made that the drainage holes are not clogged. Any needed repairs to the boxes or their supports should be made now, before the birds take occupancy.

If Sparrows are Found

When house sparrows are found nesting in a bluebird box, all nesting material in the box (including any bluebird nests that may be underneath the sparrow's nest) should be removed. It is sometimes advisable to cover the entrance hole for a few days to encourage the sparrows to look about for a new nesting site. Since interference by sparrows is a major cause of failure to attract bluebirds, keeping sparrows out of the nesting boxes is often the most important of all monitoring tasks.

If Wasps are Found

Wasps frequently nest in bird boxes, usually attaching their nest to the inside of the top board. Birds will not nest in boxes that have active wasp colonies in them. Hence the wasps should be removed—but obviously with great care. Their sting is quite painful, and may be dangerous to individuals who are allergic to bee venom. More specific information on how to rid a nesting box of wasps will be found in Chapter 9.

If Indications of Predation are Found

If bluebird eggs or nestlings less than fifteen days old have disappeared from the nest in between inspections, it is a clear sign that one of the various predators that prey upon bluebirds has paid a visit. If the nest itself is intact and it still contains any unbroken eggs or live nestlings, they should be left undisturbed and steps should be taken quickly to prevent the predator's returning to do additional harm (see Chapter 9).

If all of the eggs have disappeared from the nest or are damaged or all the nestlings are found dead or have simply disappeared, the remaining contents of the box should be removed. Consideration should be given to relocating the nesting box where it may be protected more effectively from predation. Bluebirds whose eggs or young have succumbed to predators will try to raise a new brood, but they may wisely refuse to nest in the place where the original disaster took place.

If both live and dead nestlings are discovered in the nest, the dead ones should be removed. (The parent birds usually do this themselves if the dead birds are small enough for them to handle.)

If there is No Female to Incubate the Eggs

If the female bluebird should be killed during the incubation period there is usually little hope of saving the eggs, since the male will not incubate them and the developing embryos usually die within a short time unless incubation is resumed. Sometimes there is hope, however, if quick action is taken. The chances of saving the eggs are greatest if incubation has not yet been started, which would be the case if the clutch of eggs had not been completed or had just been completed at the time the mother bird was killed, and before she had commenced incubation. The eggs would then still be viable if they are not more than about six days old. If there are other bluebird nests in the area with incomplete or just completed clutches of eggs, the eggs left by the dead bird may be placed in these other nests. It is best, however, not to overload any nest with a total of more than six eggs.

Once incubation has commenced it cannot be suspended more than a few hours without seriously endangering the embryos. If partially incubated eggs can be retrieved soon enough after incubation has been halted, they may be shifted to other nests, if there are any, where incubation has been going on for approximately the same length of time. Again, care should be taken not to overload any given nest.

Sometimes a raccoon or other predator out to get some bluebird eggs succeeds in reaching into the nesting box but only manages to disrupt the nest without actually reaching its contents. When that happens, the eggs in the nest frequently roll to the bottom of the nesting box without being broken. Nests that have been disrupted in this manner will be abandoned by the adult bluebirds and should be removed. If any unbroken eggs are retrieved quickly enough after the predator's attack and the status of the eggs (i.e., whether or not they have begun to be incubated) is known, it may be possible to save the eggs by placing them in other nests in the manner described above.

Artificial Incubation

It is possible to incubate bluebird eggs artificially and raise the young birds to maturity, but the task is sufficiently difficult and involved not to be recommended for general use and a description of it lies beyond the scope of this book. It should also be pointed out that artificial incubation technically comes under the heading of artificial propagation of wildlife, a practice which is carefully regulated by Federal law. Before artificial propagation may be conducted legally, a permit must be obtained from the Fish and Wildlife Service of the U.S. Department of the Interior.

If Abandoned Nestlings are Found

Occasionally in the course of monitoring boxes along a bluebird trail abandoned but still living nestlings may be discovered. Abandonment almost always means that both of the parent birds have died. Occasionally nestlings may be abandoned if they are too weak to open their mouths to receive the food brought to them by the parent birds. The latter situation sometimes arises during prolonged periods of unseasonably cold and wet weather, when a shortage of food, or chilling, or a combination of both weakens the nestlings to the point where they can no longer respond to the offer of food. When that happens the nestlings' condition deteriorates rapidly and in only a short time they will die of starvation. Sometimes, of course, the nestlings' weakness may be brought on by illness unconnected with the weather.

If the abandoned nestlings are still able to raise their heads and open their mouths at the time they are discovered, they should be regarded as orphans suitable for adoption by neighboring bluebirds, if there are any with nestlings of roughly the same age. Once again, care should be taken not to burden the foster parents with a total of more than six nestlings to care for.

If no bluebird foster parents are available or the abandoned nestlings are too weak to accept food, the only alternative, if they are to be saved, is to raise them by hand and release them to the wild as soon as they are capable of fending for themselves. This is an arduous and time-consuming task, although it can also be a satisfying and heartwarming one. My own firsthand experience in raising a brood of orphaned nestlings in this manner is related in Chapter 11, and some practical advice—e.g., about what to feed bluebird nestlings—will be found there. Again, as with artificial incubation of abandoned eggs, it should be stressed that the raising of wild birds by hand is regulated by law and that a permit must be sought from the Fish and Wildlife Service.

A further word of caution is in order on the designation of nestlings as "abandoned." Nestlings should not be considered abandoned unless one can be sure they have not been fed for a period of at least four daylight hours. If there is doubt about it, the only way of making sure is to observe the nest continuously for a period of four hours from a distance of fifty feet or so. Only if the nestlings are conspicuously limp and cold and barely able to move at the time of their discovery can it be assumed that they have gone unfed long enough to be classified immediately as "abandoned."

If Water is Discovered in the Nesting Box

Water sometimes accumulates in a nesting box as the result of a leaky roof or a heavy storm from the direction in which the box faces. The fact that it gets in is one thing, and may indicate a need for repairs; but if it accumulates that means the drainage holes in the floor are clogged. Run a wire or small stick up through these holes to open them.

If the nest in a box in which water has accumulated contains bluebirds less than twelve days old and the weather is cold, replacing the nest with dry grass will sometimes save the lives of the nestlings. The whole job can be done in five minutes or less. First remove the nestlings gently, placing them on some dry grass or cloth in a small box or basket, and cover them lightly with a piece of cloth or paper towel. Remove and discard the wet nest and be sure to open any clogged drainage holes in the floor of the nesting box to prevent a recurrence. Next place some clean dry grass in the box and pack it down tightly. If the nestlings are less than about nine days old the new handmade nest should be cupped in the center so that the nestlings will stay close together. A flat mat of tightly packed dry grass about an inch thick is adequate for older nestlings.

If the nestlings are very young and appear cold and weak it may help to warm them in the bare hands for a minute or two before placing them in the new nest.

Finally, close the box and leave the area as quickly as possible so that the parent birds may resume their duties with a minimum of delay.

The procedure described above should *not* be attempted if the nest contains bluebird nestlings twelve days old or older. These older nestlings should never be removed from the nest. If they are, they may become so excited by the disturbance that they will no longer remain in the nest once they are put back into it. They are not yet ready for the world, and birds that leave the nest prematurely seldom survive.

If Blowfly Infestation is Discovered

If a bluebird nest is heavily infested with blowfly larvae (see Chapter 9) and the nestlings appear to be in a weakened condition or poorly developed for their age, the nest should be removed and destroyed, and should then be replaced with dry grass as described in the preceding section.

Removal of Old Bluebird Nests

If in the course of inspection of a bluebird box a well flattened but natural-looking empty nest (i.e., one that does not appear to have been disturbed by a predator) is found, and fifteen days or more have elapsed since the eggs were hatched, it is safe to assume that nestlings have been fledged. The old nest should then be entirely discarded—but not before it has been examined. If it is found to contain large numbers of tiny crawling insects (probably bird lice) or mites, the inside of the nesting box may be dusted with a 1% rotenone powder or sprayed with a pyrethrin spray in an effort to control the infestation.

Old nests should always be removed as promptly as possible after the young birds have left, since this increases the chances that the same nesting box will be used for the next brood of the season. Removal of the old nest also increases the chances for the next brood's survival. If the original nest is not removed, bluebirds will sometimes build a new nest directly over it, and the new nest may then be high enough for starlings to be able to reach it and destroy its contents even though they cannot actually get into the nesting box. Often only a few days elapse between the time the young birds of one brood leave the nest and the start of the new nest for the next brood, which is why the old nest should be promptly removed. If the bluebirds have already begun building a new nest over the old one when the box is inspected, it is best to leave it undisturbed.

The Season's Final Monitoring

The last inspection of the nesting boxes of the season may be done at any time in the autumn, or it may be put off until the following February. Whenever it is done, the nesting boxes should be cleaned out, the drainage holes should be checked to make sure they are not clogged, and any needed repairs should be made.

Reading the Signs of a Bluebird Nest

If a nesting box has been left unwatched and undisturbed for an entire nesting season, a lot can be told from an examination of the contents at the season's end. An undisturbed nest that is well flattened and that has a slightly crusted-over look on top indicates that it once contained young birds close to the fledging age. Another thing to look for is the presence of a considerable quantity of pin-feather scales in the nesting material. These scales (which resemble dandruff) are shed by the young birds during their last few days in the nest. Without having been there to witness the fledging there is no way the observer can be sure the birds were fledged successfully; but these telltale signs of maturing nestlings raise hope that they were.

The presence of two or three such nests in the same nesting box, one over the other, indicates that two or three broods were raised during the season.

A clean, cup-shaped bluebird nest in a box at the end of the season indicates that the birds were probably unsuccessful in raising a brood in it, although a very small brood of one or two nestlings might have been raised.

A badly disarranged nest obviously is a strong indication of a predator's having attacked the nest and having in all likelihood destroyed the eggs or young birds in it.

On the other hand, the lack of visible disturbance does not necessarily indicate freedom from predation since a snake could have raided the nest and made off with the eggs or nestlings without perceptibly disturbing the nest. The presence of puparia of the parasitic blowfly in the nesting material (see Chapter 9) will give an indication of the extent of infestation by this parasite locally.

A Typical Bluebird Nesting Timetable

The following timetable will give the inexperienced reader some idea of what he or she may expect to encounter in the course of monitoring bluebird nesting boxes. The timetable shows the approximate timing of the normal sequence of events in the nesting of the eastern bluebird in Maryland. It assumes no interference by competitors, predators, or unseasonable weather. Naturally, conditions will vary somewhat for the other bluebird species and in other regions of the country. In the far south the typical sequence may run two or more weeks earlier. In the north the events may take place as much as a month later and third broods are rarely if ever encountered. In addition to regional variations, local weather conditions in early spring may retard or advance the start of the nesting season. But in the main the sequence of events may be expected to be about as described below.

February 25	Bluebirds return to their breeding areas
February 26– March 15	Birds seek out suitable nesting sites

March 15	Male bluebird locates a nesting site
March 15–17	Male tries to induce the female bluebird to accept his chosen nesting site (natural cavity or nesting box)
March 17	Female accepts the site, and in so doing accepts the male as her mate
March 17–April 8	"Honeymoon" period: the bluebird pair remains in the vicinity of the nesting site, frequently examines it, and attempts to drive away other possible occupants
April 9–13	Female bluebird builds a nest, with much encouragement from her mate
April 14–18	Pair remains in the general vicinity of the nest
April 18–22	Egg laying takes place (usually one egg each day for five days)
April 22–May 6	Incubation period: the female incubates the eggs for fourteen days, while the male remains close by, often bringing food to the female. He guards the nest while the female is out for food and exercise
May 6	Eggs hatch, and the female bird carries away the shells
May 6–23	Both adults work tirelessly from dawn to dusk to feed the nestlings. The female broods the young for shorter and shorter periods as they grow
May 23	Young bluebirds leave the nest, generally flying directly to a tree, shrub, or fence nearby on their first flight
May 24–30	Both parents continue to devote full time to the feeding and protection of the young
May 31–June 4	Female builds a new nest for the second brood, often (but not necessarily) in the same cavity or nesting box. The male continues to feed and care for the young of the first brood

June 8–11	Egg laying for the second brood (typically one egg each day for four days)
June 11–24	Incubation period: the incubation of the second brood ordinarily lasts thirteen days. Young of the first brood have now become independent, but stay nearby
June 24	Eggs hatch, and the female again carries away the shells
June 24–July 11	The young of the second brood remain in the nest and are constantly fed. (Sometimes young of the first brood assist in the feeding)
July 11	Nestlings of the second brood leave the nest (The nesting season may end here, or a third brood may be raised as described below)
July 17–22	Female bluebird builds a new nest for the third brood
July 26–28	Egg laying takes place (typically one egg each day for three days)
July 28–August 10	Incubation period: incubation of the third brood usually lasts thirteen days
August 10	Eggs hatch, and the female again carries away the shells
August 10–27	Young of the third brood remain in the nest and are constantly fed
August 27	Nestlings of the third brood leave the nest
August 27–September 17	Both parent birds and sometimes young birds of the earlier broods continue to feed the young of the third brood

Further Reading

Pinkowski, B. C. 1975. A summary and key for determining causes of nesting failures in Eastern Bluebirds using nesting boxes. *Inland Bird Banding News* 47: 179–186.

[8]
Bluebird Trails

In 1959 Dr. and Mrs. John Lane of Brandon, Manitoba, organized a boy's club known as the Brandon Junior Birders, whose members took it upon themselves to build nesting boxes and set them out along the roadside. From this modest beginning there grew what is now unquestionably the world's longest bluebird trail, a magnificent network of trails and side-trails stretching all the way from near Winnipeg, Manitoba, on the east to Saskatoon, Saskatchewan. Along its approximately 2500 miles (including numerous shorter trails that branch off from the main line) it is estimated that more than five thousand young bluebirds and ten thousand tree swallows are fledged each year.

As impressive as the Canadian trail's sheer extent is the number of individuals and groups that have joined forces during the last decade and a half to make the trail a reality, to enlarge its scope, and to ensure that the nesting boxes along it are maintained in good condition to go on fostering the welfare of bluebirds for the future.

This chapter tells about bluebird trails, what they are,

where some of them are, how they came to be, and who some of the individuals and groups are who have aided the bluebirds by helping to set up and maintain bluebird trails in various regions of North America. Only a few of the people who have pioneered in establishing bluebird trails can be mentioned here. In the example they and others who must go unnamed have set, lies the bluebirds' hope for the future. If enough others follow that example, bluebird trails will one day crisscross the continent and bluebirds will again be a familiar sight in places where most people have forgotten that they ever existed.

What Makes a Bluebird Trail?

A bluebird trail consists of a number of bluebird nesting boxes, usually spaced a hundred yards or more apart, put in suitable locations and arranged in such a manner that they may be monitored conveniently by someone going from box to box by car, by bicycle, or on foot. Since making the rounds of the boxes is obviously more efficient if the trail is roughly circular, trails are often laid out in that manner. The minimum number of nesting boxes along a trail might be half a dozen or so. There is no upper limit, of course. Some of the larger trails, along which the nesting boxes number in the hundreds, even thousands, are cooperative ventures. Responsibility for monitoring the boxes along them is usually divided among different individuals or groups through whose localities the trails make their way.

A 8o-acre farm can usually support a bluebird trail of two dozen or so nesting boxes around its border. More extensive trails may be laid out on large farms or ranches or along country roads where use may sometimes be made of utility poles, fence posts, etc., to support the boxes—after permission has been obtained from the utility companies or property owners involved.

Golf courses often provide excellent bluebird habitat unless they are too close to cities and towns. They usually have the combination of scattered trees, open areas, and short grass that bluebirds find so congenial. On a golf course bluebird trail the nesting boxes should be set out in the "rough" areas well off the fairways or in the long narrow areas with scattered trees that often separate adjacent fairways. An 18-hole golf course may be able to support a bluebird trail of up to seventy-five nesting boxes.

If a trail is being established on a private golf course, it is a good idea to enlist the interest of the members by explaining the purpose of the trail. For many golfers, the trail will be a source of added interest on the course. A friend of mine who is an ardent golfer as well as a bluebird enthusiast has doubled the pleasure of his game by monitoring his bluebird trail while golfing (of course allowing other golfers to "play through").

Numbering the nesting boxes along a bluebird trail will simplify record keeping, and attaching a small plate or plastic label to each box to show the name of the person or organization responsible for the trail may help to discourage vandalism. One local Rotary Club, for example, attaches a Rotary International insignia to each of its nesting boxes. A prominent bluebird trail operator in Illinois affixes a card to each box bearing the following message:

Please help me save the bluebirds for posterity
Ralph M. J. Shook
Route 6, Godfrey, Illinois 62035

Developing a Successful Trail

Immediate success in establishing a trail is most likely to come where bluebirds have been seen fairly frequently in recent years, of course. But you should not feel discouraged from attempting to aid the bluebirds in re-establishing themselves in any otherwise suitable rural area simply because no bluebirds have been seen there recently. If no bluebirds at all have been seen in a particular area for a year or more, it might be wise to begin modestly, setting out only a few boxes the first year and then increasing their number annually as the bluebird population itself increases. There have been numerous reports of bluebird boxes that have been occupied during the first season they were up even though no one could recall having seen bluebirds in the vicinity for ten years or more. The few bluebirds that may still be in the region will, if necessary, conduct an exhaustive search over a wide area in late winter or early spring for suitable nesting sites.

Once a few pairs of bluebirds are re-established in an area the population can often be increased quite impressively in that area within only a few years by gradual development and extension of the bluebird trail; since the young birds often remain in or return to the same general area to nest.

Operating bluebird trails is a fascinating hobby for individuals and a worthy and rewarding project for organizations such as bird clubs, garden clubs, golf clubs, 4-H Clubs, Boy Scouts, Girl Scouts, Camp Fire Girls, and service organizations. Successful trails should obviously be maintained indefinitely, and if possible increased in size as the local bluebird population grows. When bluebird trails are unsuccessful the blame may usually be traced to either improper location of the nesting boxes or failure to prevent house sparrows from taking over the boxes. One of the gratifying features of bluebird trails as conservation projects is their very high success rate. Well-planned and properly monitored trails in good bluebird habitat virtually always succeed unless they are in areas where bluebirds have completely disappeared. The ones now in existence have proved to be sources of great pleasure to those responsible for them.

Origin of Bluebird Trails

The trail set in motion in Canada in 1959 may be considered the most impressive culmination to date of the bluebird conservation work begun some forty years ago by Dr. T. E. Musselman of Quincy, Illinois, who is credited with having originated both the concept and the name of "bluebird trails." Bluebird conservation antedates Dr. Musselman, but he was a pioneer in putting it on an organized footing.

In 1934 Dr. Musselman set out 25 bluebird nesting boxes along country roads in Adams County, Illinois. By that date bluebirds had already become quite scarce there, as in many other places. Later he increased his trail to more than a hundred boxes spread along some 43 miles of country roads. Within a few years the bluebird population had increased spectacularly all along the route of the trail. Encouraged by the continuing success of his project, Dr. Musselman in more recent years has expanded his activities and is devoting much of his efforts to encouraging, advising, and helping others in establishing new bluebird trails in many parts of the country.

Other Leaders in Bluebird Conservation

Among other bluebird trail pioneers should be mentioned the late Seth Low [1934], who operated a trail on Cape Cod in Massachusetts, and the late Amelia R. Laskey [1939, 1940, 1956] of Nashville, Tennessee, who started a highly successful bluebird trail at Percy Warner Park in 1936. Mrs. Laskey and John S. Herbert [1968, 1969, 1971, 1972] launched another equally successful trail along rural roads near Ashland City, Tennessee, in 1968.

William L. Highhouse [1964] of Warren, Pennsylvania, has maintained an active bluebird project known as "Operation Bluebird" in Warren County, Pennsylvania, since 1957. By 1974 he and some thirty others who have helped to maintain and monitor the "Operation Bluebird" nesting boxes had mounted approximately four hundred boxes along some one hundred miles of Warren County roads. During that one year alone, a total of 867 eastern bluebirds and 532 tree swallows were fledged from "Operation Bluebird's" nesting boxes.

Elsewhere in Pennsylvania, Ralph K. Bell [1968] of Clarksville has maintained a successful bluebird trail along the country roads of the southwestern part of the state since 1964. As many as eight hundred or more bluebirds are fledged annually from his nesting boxes, which number more than two hundred.

In Illinois, Ralph M. J. Shook of Godfrey, remembering the abundance of bluebirds in his native Calhoun County during his boyhood, became appalled by how scarce they had become by 1970. Determined to do whatever he could to remedy the situation, he began building nesting boxes which he then set out in rural areas. Some he gave away to others who promised to mount them in proper locations. By 1973 nearly five hundred of his nesting boxes had been set out, roughly half of them were occupied by bluebirds, and the sadly depleted bluebird population of Illinois' Calhoun County was making a substantial comeback.

Mention has already been made of the magnificent trail that traverses the Canadian prairie provinces of Saskatchewan and Manitoba, originated by the Lanes and the Brandon (Manitoba) Junior Birders (Lane [1971, 1972] and Lane and Martin [1973]). By 1973 their trail extended from Peace Garden, Manitoba, on the south to Ste. Rose and Russell on the north, and from MacGregor on the east to Broadview, Saskatchewan, on the west. At this point it joins the trail operated by Lorne Scott [1970, 1971, 1972] of Indian Head, Saskatchewan, which extends west and north to Raymore, where it in turn joins the trail operated by Dr. Stuart Houston and the Saskatoon Junior Natural History Society. More than seven thousand nesting boxes are mounted along this mammoth combined trail or network of trails, and more than five thousand young bluebirds and ten thousand young tree swallows are fledged from them annually. Most of the bluebirds in this region are mountain bluebirds, but a considerable number of eastern bluebirds are also found near the eastern end of the trail. Several instances of cross breeding between the two species have been reported (Lane [1969]).

In another part of Canada, through the combined efforts of Leo Smith of Toronto, the Oshawa Naturalist Club, the Willow Beach Field Naturalist Club, and the Ontario Bird Banding Association, several extensive bluebird trails have been established in southern Ontario with a total of about twelve hundred nesting boxes.

The Grand Rapids Audubon Club organized a "Bluebirds Unlimited" project in 1962. Under the able leadership of Raleigh R. Stotz of Grand Rapids, Michigan, this organization established an experimental bluebird trail at Gun Lake and has devoted much time and effort to educational activities in the field of bluebird conservation. Educational materials concerning bluebirds are distributed by the Club in great quantities, advice is supplied to many individuals and organizations interested in joining the bluebird conservation movement, and nearly fifteen thousand bluebird nesting boxes have been sold virtually at cost.

The National Association for the Protection and Propagation of the Purple Martins and Bluebirds of America in 1968 published instructions for making and setting out bluebird nesting boxes and a booklet entitled "Bluebirds for Posterity" (Zeleny [1968]). Some seven thousand copies of the instructions and four thousand copies of the booklet were sold within a few years, resulting in the establishment of a number of new bluebird trails around the country. In 1969 the Association's work passed into the hands of the Griggsville Wild Bird Society of Griggsville, Illinois, which publishes the *Purple Martin News*, a widely distributed monthly periodical which treats a wide range of conservation topics in a popular style. Each issue of the *Purple Martin News* features a monthly column entitled "The Bluebird Trail."

William G. Duncan of Louisville, Kentucky, has been actively engaged in bluebird conservation work for many years and has supplied nesting box plans, printed material about bluebirds, and advice on the development of bluebird trails to interested people throughout the country.

The Audubon Naturalist Society of the Central Atlantic States (ANS) launched a bluebird project in 1967 (Zeleny [1967]) that was subsequently partially integrated with a similar project begun two years later by the Maryland Ornithological Society (MOS). A goal of the combined project was to interest both members and friends of the two organizations who owned or had access to rural property in setting out and maintaining bluebird nesting boxes. As a result, some seventy-five collaborators have been enlisted, including some who have established their own bluebird trails. By 1975 some sixteen hundred nesting boxes were being maintained by the people participating in the joint project, and nearly four thousand bluebirds were fledged from the boxes that year (Zeleny [1975]). In most of the areas in which trails developed under the joint auspices of the ANS and the MOS have been in operation for several years, remarkable increases in the local bluebird population have been noted.

A further and perhaps even more fruitful activity growing out of this joint project has been in the educational field. Many lectures and demonstrations have been presented to bird clubs, garden clubs, service and youth organizations, and other groups. Following publicity through the major communications media an estimated twelve thousand sets of plans for bluebird nesting boxes and instructions for their use prepared by the Maryland Ornithological Society were distributed over a two-year period to people who requested them, and hundreds of letters seeking additional information have been received. The Society's success in drawing attention to the bluebird conservation movement through press releases, announcements over local television stations, and other publicity efforts suggests that similar efforts on the part of other groups across the country could easily lead to a multiplication of the number of people interested in becoming involved in the establishment of bluebird trails.

The author's own bluebird trail (Zeleny [1971b]), operated as part of the joint ANS-MOS project, is located on the grounds of the Agricultural Research Center of the U.S. Department of Agriculture, a 13,000-acre tract near Beltsville, Maryland (about seven miles north of Washington, D.C., and quite close to heavily populated suburban developments). This particular trail is of interest because it demonstrates what can be done to re-establish bluebirds near the fringe of a major metropolitan area where starlings are the predominant species of bird throughout the breeding season.

Prior to 1950 bluebirds were fairly common at the Agricultural Research Center despite a heavy population of house sparrows. The bluebirds nested in natural cavities as far as possible from buildings and other places where sparrows congregated. Practically no starlings nested in the vicinity up to that time. Shortly after 1950, however, starlings began moving into the area in large numbers. By the late 1950s they had become the most numerous species of bird. Bluebirds had virtually disappeared, and for the next ten years were rarely seen in the area.

The Beltsville trail was started in 1967 with moderate success and has been expanded during each subsequent year. In spite of heavy local populations of house sparrows and starlings, some two hundred young bluebirds were fledged along the trail during each of the years from 1970 through 1975, showing that even in areas where the bluebirds' cause may appear to be lost there is hope for the future.

Further Reading

Kibler, L. F. 1969. The establishment and maintenance of a bluebird nest-box project. A review and commentary. *Bird-Banding* 40: 114–129.

McKnight, E. T. 1973. A nest box project for bluebirds in Stafford County, Virginia. *The Raven* 44: 59–68.

Musselman, T. E. 1935. Three years of Eastern Bluebird banding and study. *Bird-Banding* 6: 117–125.

Terres, J. K. 1968. *Songbirds in Your Garden*. New York: Thomas Y. Crowell Co. Chapter 10.

[9]

Coping with the Bluebird's Enemies

THIS CHAPTER is concerned mainly with predators that attack bluebirds and how their toll can be minimized by careful management of bluebird nesting boxes and trails. For nearly all species of wildlife predators are an ever-present threat. Predation is one of nature's ways of maintaining ecological balance by preventing a species from becoming so populous that it becomes a threat to other wildlife as well as to its own survival. In the course of evolution species have of necessity developed means of defending themselves against their natural enemies. By the process of natural selection those individual members of a species equipped with the best means of survival are the ones most likely to live to produce offspring that will in turn perpetuate those characteristics. Porcupines, rattlesnakes, and skunks are familiar examples of species that have developed unusual and effective defenses against animals that would prey on them. Animals and birds that have been unable to develop adequate defenses have fallen by the evolutionary wayside and joined the long list of extinct species. Man, of course, is the greatest enemy of all and many wildlife species have been unable to cope with his ruthless behavior.

Bluebirds, like other birds, have always had to contend with predators, especially the kinds that seek out their nests in order to eat their eggs and nestlings. Bluebirds are one of those birds that at some remote point in evolutionary time sought refuge from predators by building their nests in natural cavities, where the eggs and young could not so readily be seen. Moreover, in uneven combat the birds would have a better chance of defending their nests against attack when they were lodged in cavities. Various predators still found it possible to raid bluebird nests, at least some of the time, but the cavity-nesting strategy served the bluebirds well on the whole and they were able to maintain a good population despite losses by predation—until the advent of house sparrows and starlings.

At present the most urgent need of the bluebirds is for starling-proof nesting boxes of the kind described elsewhere in this book (see Chapter 5). But for bluebirds to re-establish themselves where their numbers have dwindled it is obviously desirable to protect their nests as well as we can against enemies of all kinds. A wide range of creatures including mammals, reptiles, birds, and insects prey upon or otherwise interfere with the bluebirds while they are endeavoring to raise their young.

Mammalian Predators

RACCOONS

(Procyon lotor)

These beautiful, intelligent, and widely distributed animals are probably the major mammalian predators that prey upon nesting bluebirds. A raccoon can—and will—climb just about any tree or post it can maintain a grip upon to get at a bluebird nesting cavity or box, and once there it can usually manage to reach through the opening to pull out the eggs or nestlings inside, often removing part of the nest itself in the process. Occasionally raccoons even kill the adult bluebirds in the course of a raid.

What are the telltale signs of raccoon predation? If a bluebird nest is found to be badly disrupted, with perhaps part of it stringing out the entrance hole, a raccoon may be suspected. Usually the raccoon carries away its prey. Sometimes, however, the remains of the nestlings or adult bird may be discovered on the ground near the nest. If there were eggs in the nest but the raccoon was unable to reach them, the eggs may have spilled out and will then be found at the bottom of the box, beneath the disrupted nest.

The Grand Rapids Audubon Club [1974] has made a careful study of the raccoon problem along bluebird trails and concluded that the best way to foil these and other mammalian predators is to mount the nesting boxes on smooth metal fence posts or angle iron posts. Galvanized water pipes are also good for this purpose. Raccoons can climb untreated metal posts or pipes, however,

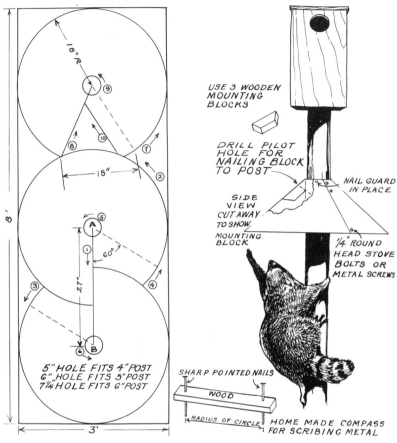

20. Conical sheet metal guard for protecting nest structures from predators.

At left is layout for cutting three predator guards from a 3 by 8-foot sheet of 26–gauge galvanized metal. When installing the guard, overlap cut edge to dotted line. See hole sizes. To facilitate cutting (on solid lines only) follow sequence of numbers. Make circular cuts in counterclockwise direction. To make initial cut on line A–B, make slot at A with a cold chisel for inserting shears. (*Courtesy U.S. Fish and Wildlife Service*)

21. Typical evidence of raccoon predation

so a heavy coating of soft automobile grease (often sold as "all-purpose" grease) should be applied. The application must be repeated several times during the nesting season because the grease tends to harden with age—making the posts easier to climb than if no grease at all had been applied to them. The Grand Rapids Audubon Club maintains a bluebird trail in an area in which raccoons are quite populous. Since greased metal posts have been used for mounting the nesting boxes the Club reports that not a single nest has been disturbed by raccoons, which had previously raided from twenty to twenty-five percent of the nests.

Webster and Uhler [1964] have experimented with various devices for keeping raccoons and other climbing predators out of wood duck nesting boxes. The most effective device proved to be a large conical guard made of sheet metal attached to the post on which the nesting box is mounted. Detailed instructions for making and installing this type of guard are given in Figure 20.

A somewhat simpler "sandwich type" sheet metal guard suitable for use on metal posts is also recommended by the same investigators. This guard is made from a 38″ x 18″ sheet of 24 gauge (0.02″ thick) moderately soft sheet aluminum. The sheet is folded tightly in half lengthwise to form a double thickness 38″ x 9″. The post is then enclosed centrally between the two halves of the aluminum sheet and the two 38″ edges are riveted together. Finally, the guard is bolted or wired securely to the post (see Fig. 22).

The latter type of guard was found initially to be fully effective against raccoons. Later studies showed that some raccoons eventually do learn to climb these guards by grasping both edges, using all four feet, and hunching themselves upwards an inch or so at a time. Bluebird nesting boxes may offer less incentive than wood duck boxes to the raccoons to master this difficult climbing skill. The guards are said to be effective against all other common climbing predators.

Because of the cost and labor involved, the foregoing methods for controlling raccoons and other mammalian predators may be impractical in some instances. This is especially likely to be the case for many extensive bluebird trails, along which nesting boxes are often mounted on the posts of existing fences or on utility poles. Where permission has to be sought from private landowners, it may be difficult to get permission to set up special posts for the nesting boxes, even if cost and labor are not a consideration. Simpler methods of predator control must then be used even though they may be less reliable.

The most commonly used simple "coon guard" consists of a small board with a hole 1½″ in diameter nailed or screwed to the outside of the front board of the nesting box so that the hole coincides with the entrance hole of the box. A board 4″ wide and as long as the width of the box is adequate for this purpose (see Fig. 23). The combined thickness of this board and the front board of the box should be at least 1½″. It is very difficult for a raccoon or other large mammal to reach through an opening of that depth and down to the bluebird nest. However, when bluebirds build a higher than normal nest, or build a second or third nest on top of previous

Predator guard made from sheet aluminum 38″ x 18″. The sheet is folded tightly lengthwise to form a a double panel 38″ x 9″. This is placed around the metal support post and the free edges riveted or bolted together as shown. The guard is then bolted or wired securely to the post.

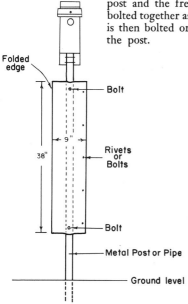

22. "Sandwich Type" Sheet Metal Predator Guard

23. Nesting box fitted with a wooden raccoon guard

ones that have not been removed, the guard becomes ineffective.

Although the kind of guard described above is more effective in discouraging predators if it is thicker, unfortunately it also appears that bluebirds find entrance holes deeper than 1½″ or so less acceptable.

Protection against raccoons can also be provided by deeper nesting boxes (see Fig. 15), i.e., ones in which the distance from the bottom of the entrance hole to the floor is eight or even ten inches instead of the usual six. Here again, however, the effectiveness of such a deep box is occasionally defeated by the birds themselves, when they build their nests high enough to be reached by predators through the entrance hole. Extra-deep nesting boxes fitted with the kind of raccoon guard described above may be a good solution in areas where raccoons pose a serious threat, if the more effective sheet metal guards cannot be used.*

Charles W. McQuillin of Zurich, Ontario, has found the ten inch deep boxes to be quite effective in his area, and suggests attaching a piece of sheet metal to the front of the box surrounding the entrance hole to discourage raccoons from gnawing at the wood as they sometimes do.

OPOSSUMS

(Didelphis marsupialis)

Opossums, the only North American marsupials, are known to rob birds' nests. They are very likely guilty of having preyed upon bluebirds although there are no definite observations of their having done so. The same methods described above for the protection of bluebird nests from raccoon predation would be effective against opossums, perhaps even more so than against raccoons.

, * See page 55 for precautions applicable to extra-deep nesting boxes in areas where tree swallows or violet-green swallows nest.

HOUSE CATS

Although they sometimes raid bluebird nests in the same manner as raccoons, house cats are a greater threat to both young and adult bluebirds out of the nest than in the nest. Bluebirds feed mainly from the ground, usually alighting on the ground momentarily to snatch insects they have spotted from overhead perches. Cats will take note of the bluebirds' favorite feeding spots and hide in nearby underbrush, motionless, waiting with extraordinary patience to pounce on any bird that alights within range. Young bluebirds that fail to reach a tree or other safe haven at the time they are fledged stand a good chance of falling prey to cats that happen to be in the vicinity. In a sense this is nature's way of weeding out the weaklings of a species. But strictly speaking house cats do not qualify as natural enemies, since they are not native to the areas in which bluebirds are found.

In general, the methods that are effective against raccoons will also protect bluebird nests from predation by cats. It should be remembered, however, that some house cats are able to leap six feet or more straight up from the ground. In areas where cats are a serious threat to bluebirds, it may be necessary to mount the nesting boxes higher than six feet, no matter how the posts are treated or equipped to control climbing predators.

SQUIRRELS

Squirrels of various species can be a great nuisance when nesting boxes are located close to wooded areas, especially if the boxes are mounted on trees or unprotected wooden posts. Most squirrels can climb metal posts but are not likely to do so if the posts are kept thickly coated with grease. The sheet metal guards described above are also effective against squirrels. Squirrels do not ordinarily bother nesting boxes on fences around open fields.

The red squirrel (*Tamiasciurus hudsonicus*) seems to be the worst offender of the group. These little busybodies will enter bluebird nesting boxes, gnawing away some of the wood to gain entrance if necessary, and eat the bluebird eggs or nestlings, even killing an adult bluebird occasionally in the process.

Gray squirrels (*Sciurus carolinensis and S. griseus*) may also cause trouble although they seldom rob bluebirds of their eggs or young. If a nesting box is mounted on a tree these squirrels will often remodel it to suit their own needs by enlarging the entrance hole so that they can come and go with ease. If the box is sufficiently large they will build nests of their own in it and raise their young there. The small bluebird box (the one with a floor measuring 4″ x 4″) is too small for the gray squirrel to nest in; but with an enlarged entranceway it does make cozy sleeping quarters for a squirrel on rainy days or cold winter nights.

The tiny nocturnal flying squirrels (*Glaucomys* sp.) have easy access to bluebird nesting boxes. Boxes that are close to wooded areas may be found attractive by flying squirrels for raising their families. They build their nests in late winter, before the bluebirds have returned to nest, and the young squirrels occupy the boxes during most of the period when bluebirds might otherwise be raising their first broods of the season in them. I have never known flying squirrels to prey on bluebird eggs or nestlings but cannot be sure that they are as innocent as they look. When monitoring bluebird trails I have never had the heart to evict flying squirrels when they look up at me with their huge trusting eyes. In my eyes these friendly little animals are among the most beautiful and appealing of all living creatures. Greased poles are to no avail. But if the boxes are placed at some distance from wooded areas they are unlikely to be taken over by flying squirrels.

CHIPMUNKS

Chipmunks occasionally enter nesting boxes and raid the nests, but this is likely to be a problem only when the local chipmunk population is relatively high and their food supply is relatively low. Adult bluebirds are able to defend their nests against these intruders and usually do unless they are caught napping. The greased metal posts or sheet metal guards recommended for protection against raccoons will also keep chipmunks down.

MICE

White-footed mice (*Peromyscus leucopus*) and other related species frequently find bluebird nesting boxes to their liking as nesting sites. When making the rounds of the boxes in February or March for their spring house-cleaning, you may find some of the boxes nearly full of very loosely packed grass or other fine plant material. If you then plunge your hand in to clean out the material, you may come up with a handful of squeaking balls of soft, clean fur violently protesting your intrusion. Also some of your fingers may be gently nipped. If evicted, these beautiful little mice are quick to take the hint and will soon relocate elsewhere. Consequently they are seldom a problem by the time the bluebirds are ready to build their nests.

Predatory Snakes

Snakes are among the most serious bluebird predators during the nesting season, particularly in the southern half of the United States. Virtually all climbing snakes probably rob bluebird nests of their eggs and young at times. The principal offenders seem to be the various subspecies of racer snakes of the species *Coluber constrictor* and the rat snakes of the species *Elaphe obsoleta*.

Snakes swallow bluebird eggs or young birds whole, and will sometimes even trap and swallow one of the adult birds. A large snake can consume an entire brood of nearly full-grown nestlings at a single meal. To get at the eggs or nestlings, a snake may intrude itself just far enough into the box to reach them; or it may enter completely.

Sometimes in the course of inspecting a nesting box one may come upon a snake coiled inside the box in a stuporous condition, waiting for its meal to digest. The number of birds consumed can often be determined by counting the clearly visible lumps on the snake's body.

When bluebird eggs or nestlings too young to be fledged have disappeared from a nest and the nest itself is undisturbed, and no traces of broken eggs or the remains of the nestlings can be found on the ground, it is almost certain that the culprit was either a snake or a two-legged predator. The two types of sheet metal guards previously described for controlling raccoons are said to be effective against snakes. Greased poles provide some protection, but there have been many reports of snakes that have climbed right through freshly applied grease. Oil of creosote liberally applied to a band of absorbent material wrapped around the post evidently deters some snakes. But again, there have been reliable reports of snakes that were not deterred by such a barrier.

Predatory Birds

Hawks, owls, crows, jays, magpies, and grackles are the birds that ordinarily come to mind when predatory birds are mentioned. Some of these birds do, on occasion, prey on smaller adult birds (including bluebirds) or on the eggs and nestlings of other species of birds, any of which they may use for food. None of these predators is a significant threat to bluebird eggs or nestlings, however, since they are unable to enter the cavities or nesting boxes normally used by the bluebirds. Only three species of cavity-nesters commonly resort to the destruction of bluebird eggs or nestlings. These three species may therefore be considered predators even though they do not actually feed upon the eggs or young that they destroy.

STARLINGS

Wherever starlings are abundant and bluebirds are forced to depend upon natural cavities for nesting sites, the starlings are unquestionably the number one enemy of the bluebirds. Starlings will take possession of virtually all of the natural cavities that bluebirds could use and they will destroy the bluebirds' eggs and nestlings if necessary in order to dominate the cavity supply. Luckily, the threat thus posed to the bluebirds may be almost completely eliminated by the provision of starling-proof bluebird nesting boxes in sufficient quantities. No other means of starling control is necessary on bluebird trails, although it should be mentioned that starlings are not protected by law.

HOUSE SPARROWS

In areas where both starlings and house sparrows are present in large numbers, house sparrows under natural conditions are second only to starlings as enemies of the bluebirds. When the starling problem has been brought under control by the use of starling-proof nesting boxes, the house sparrows then become the bluebirds' greatest enemy. Like starlings, they behave not only as fierce competitors but also as predators.

At present, there is no known design of nesting box that bluebirds can use which will effectively discourage house sparrows from moving in. It is possible, however, to control the house sparrow population in limited areas by using any of the several kinds of sparrow traps that are available commercially (see Fig. 24). The sparrows

24. One type of commercial sparrow trap

are caught unharmed and may be transported elsewhere or otherwise disposed of, since they are not protected by law. Some cautionary remarks on the use of sparrow traps are in order, however. Above all, they should be used only by people who can distinguish with certainty house sparrows from the various native sparrows and other birds that may be caught. Moreover, the traps should be set only when they can be visited at least hourly for the identification and release of any birds other than house sparrows that may enter them.

It is sometimes possible to trap house sparrows in nesting boxes while they are building their nests. If the female is caught and disposed of, the male will maintain control of the box and seek a new mate, often obtaining one on the same day. If the male sparrow is destroyed, however, the female usually abandons the box and blue-birds will then have a chance to use it.

Since house sparrows start to nest a week or more earlier in the spring than bluebirds, it is sometimes desirable to cover the entrances of the boxes until bluebirds are actually seen in the area—otherwise the bluebirds may discover no nesting sites available when they arrive and will then give up the area to search elsewhere. Obviously, careful observation and timing are required to ensure that the covers are removed as soon as the bluebirds arrive.

What if house sparrows do move into a bluebird box? Their nests should be removed at least weekly. Daily removal would be even better. Sparrows are remarkably persistent. They will frequently start rebuilding within five minutes after their nests are removed, and a pair of them may rebuild their nest as many as eight times in a row before giving up.

In the mid-Atlantic states house sparrows generally lose interest in nesting boxes by mid-July if they have not managed to occupy them earlier in the season. Bluebirds—which start to build nests as late as early August—may then be able to use the boxes for late broods without interference from sparrows.

A friend of mine had some success with an unusual ploy for warding off sparrows. When a lifelike toy snake was left in a nesting box that sparrows had persisted in using—its head positioned just inside the entrance to the box—the sparrows fled upon their return to the box and never returned. Their nest and the toy snake were then promptly removed, and before long a pair of bluebirds were happily established in the box. But in all likelihood the presence of the toy snake would have had the same effect on the bluebirds as it had on the sparrows, so a tactic of this kind requires careful timing.

As previously noted, bluebird boxes with a small (4″ x 4″) floor are somewhat less acceptable to house sparrows than larger boxes. If the boxes are mounted as low as three feet from the ground that, too, discourages the sparrows somewhat. But neither of these measures provides really effective sparrow control. It does help considerably to position the nesting boxes as far as possible from buildings, since sparrows have a marked preference for staying close to human habitations.

HOUSE WRENS

Except for starlings and house sparrows all of the birds that compete with bluebirds for nesting sites are native species. All of these native birds with the possible exception of the house wren (*Troglodytes aedon*) are highly desirable species and deserve as much encouragement and protection as we can give them. If they use our nesting boxes we should welcome them and set out additional boxes for the bluebirds. But what about the house wren? Why should we have any reservations about this smallest and most cheerful of all the birds that are likely to use our nesting boxes? After all, it is a useful insectivorous bird, and one that delights everyone with its loud bubbling song and its willingness to raise its family within arm's reach of our back doors and windows.

Unfortunately the house wren, despite its many virtues, has some very bad habits. The male of the species shows unlimited enthusiasm both as a singer and as a nest builder. He will often build a nest in every vacant cavity or nesting box within his chosen territory, and if he does not actually build nests in all of them he nonetheless fills them all with twigs, rendering them unusable by other cavity-nesting birds in the vicinity. Even though he and his mate may have no intention of using more than one of these nests, he will defend all of them furiously against other birds that try to use the nesting sites.

The house wren's worst characteristic, however, is that it sometimes slips surreptitiously into the nests of bluebirds and other cavity-nesting birds at moments when the adult birds are off guard and destroys their eggs, sometimes even killing their newly hatched nestlings. The wrens may either leave the punctured eggs or dead nestlings in the nest or throw them out onto the ground. Although bluebirds appear to be the most frequent victims of depredation of this kind, the eggs and young of entire purple martin colonies have also been known to be destroyed by individual house wrens.

It would be wrong to stigmatize all house wrens because depredations of the kind just described sometimes take place. House wrens have often been observed nesting within as little as twenty-five or fifty feet of active bluebird and chickadee nests and purple martin colonies without the least conflict. But on some bluebird trails house wrens have evidently been the most serious problem encountered. The seriousness of the problem seems to vary considerably according to local conditions.

Bluebirds are relatively safe from attack by wrens

while they are raising the first brood of the season, since in most parts of the country the early broods are well under way by the time wrens return from the south. Later bluebird broods are more vulnerable.

Since house wrens prefer to nest close to shrubbery or underbrush whereas bluebirds prefer locations that are more open, where wrens are a problem it makes sense to keep bluebird boxes out in the open. Some of the pressure from wrens may also be eliminated by placing special boxes for the wrens in brushy areas, close to shrubbery, or among the branches of trees, all places where wrens like to nest. Wren boxes may have openings as small as $1\frac{5}{16}''$ in diameter.

It should be noted that unlike starlings and house sparrows, house wrens are fully protected by Federal and many State laws. The best way to cope with them in areas where they repeatedly harass the bluebirds is to move the bluebird boxes into more open areas.

COWBIRDS

The widely distributed brown-headed cowbird (*Molothrus ater*) and the less well known bronzed cowbird (*Tangavius aeneus*) of the southwest are the only truly parasitic birds found in North America. Strictly speaking these birds are not predators, yet their actions result in the death of innumerable nestlings of other species. Cowbirds never incubate their own eggs or rear their own young. Instead, they lay their eggs in the nests of other birds, usually smaller species, most of which accept these eggs and hatch them along with their own. Since the cowbird eggs hatch in a shorter time and their nestlings mature faster than those of the other species, the cowbird nestlings are generally larger than those of the host birds. Inevitably they crowd the rightful nestlings and compete disproportionately for the food supplied by the foster parents. Frequently only the cowbird nestlings survive to be fledged. It is common to see such birds as chipping sparrows, song sparrows, and various warblers feeding young cowbirds, but no young of their own, after fledging.

Bluebirds that have built their nests in cavities with uncommonly large openings are sometimes imposed upon in this manner by cowbirds. Although the female cowbird probably could squeeze through the 1½" opening of a properly designed bluebird nesting box and there have been scattered unconfirmed reports of its happening, I have never seen an occurence of it, and it seems safe to say that cowbirds do not pose a major threat to bluebirds.

Insect Problems

Certain insects may be troublesome to bluebirds during the nesting period. Some may actually prevent the bluebirds or any birds at all from using the nesting boxes. Others are external parasites that attack and sometimes weaken the nestlings. Still others occasionally destroy and consume newly hatched nestlings.

The various types of parasites that infest birds are described by Watson and Amerson [1967].

USE OF INSECTICIDES

As a general rule the use of insecticides on wild birds or their nests should be avoided. Many are dangerous to the birds themselves. The birds may appear to tolerate a particular insecticide, yet the possibility of hidden injury must be considered. In some cases the judicious use of carefully chosen insecticides may make the difference between nesting success and failure. The potential benefit must always be weighed against known and perhaps unknown potential for harm. Before using any insecticide, read the label carefully to see if it gives instructions for use on birds or their surroundings, as required by Environmental Protection Agency regulations.

The insecticides least likely to be harmful to birds are the following:

1. *Rotenone, 1% powder.* This is a common insecticide, widely used in vegetable gardening and available at most garden supply stores. (It should be noted that although rotenone is not very toxic to birds it may be lethal to fish.)

2. *Pyrethrum powder:* Often difficult to obtain, this consists of the dried heads of any of several Old World chrysanthemums.

3. *Pyrethrins* (oily liquid esters, originally derived from chrysanthemums but now available in synthetic form): Pyrethrins are usually combined with piperonyl butoxide and other relatively safe ingredients, in aerosol spray cans. Special formulations intended for use with caged birds are available in pet supply stores. Stronger pyrethrin formulations may be used in *empty* nesting boxes. One of the newer synthetic pyrethrins is designated simply "SBP 1382."

PARASITIC BLOWFLIES

The most serious insect parasites of the bluebirds are the bluebird blowfly *Protocalliphora sialia* (also known as *Apaulina sialia*) and several closely related species. Although these blowflies attack various kinds of birds, they seem to prefer birds that nest in cavities, especially bluebirds and tree swallows.

The adult female blowfly enters the cavity or nesting box while the birds are nesting and lays her eggs in the nesting material. The eggs soon hatch and the larvae or maggots attach themselves to the baby birds and suck their blood. After they have gorged themselves sufficiently they burrow into the nesting material and remain there until maturity. Inactive at this stage and surrounded by a flexible membrane, they resemble small, dark brown eggs about ⅜″ long. Each consists of a pupa surrounded by a pupal case or puparium. After about twelve days the adult blowflies emerge from the puparia and fly away in search of fresh bird nests where they will be able to repeat the life cycle.

During the day, blowfly larvae are seldom seen on bluebird nestlings. The larvae usually attack the nestlings at night and hide in the nesting material during the daylight hours—a cycle that no doubt developed through long evolution, as those larvae that fed on the nestlings during the day would be more likely to be eaten by the adult birds, whereas the ones that fed only at night had a better chance of surviving to reproduce themselves.

Bluebird nestlings are usually able to survive the attack of parasitic blowflies and are free of infestation by the time they leave the nest. If the infestation is heavy, however, the young birds may be seriously weakened from loss of blood. This may be a contributory cause of death for young birds both within the nest and after they have left the nest, especially during cold wet weather when food is scarce. Very heavy infestation—evidenced

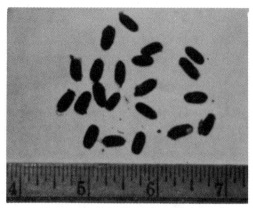

25. Puparia of bluebird parasitic blowfly

by counts of more than 150 blowfly larvae in a nest—may kill the young birds outright.

Blowfly infestation, unless it is very heavy, may usually be ignored since it does no noticeable harm to the birds. Where infestation is heavy enough to weaken the birds, it may usually be controlled by dusting the nests with 1% rotenone powder or with powdered pyrethrum. The dusting may be done before or after the eggs have been laid, but before they have hatched. If it is necessary to treat a nest after the young birds have hatched, the nestlings should be lifted gently from the nest before the application, and the insecticide should be worked carefully into the nesting material with the finger so that as little of it as possible will come into contact with the nestlings when they are put back. Heavily infested nests may also be replaced by clean, dry grass in the manner suggested on pp. 85–86.

The old saying that "every flea has its own fleas"

applies well to the parasitic blowfly. A tiny wasp, *Nasonia vitripennis*, is a parasite that preys on the parasitic blowfly as well as on other flies. This wasp lays its eggs on the blowfly puparia, and the wasp larvae then develop within the puparia and devour the developing blowflies. Adult wasps rather than adult blowflies then emerge from the blowfly puparia. Obviously the presence of this tiny wasp is beneficial to the bluebirds.

Because there is no way of knowing whether blow-flies or wasps will emerge from the blowfly puparia that may be found in a bluebird nest, it is difficult to know whether or not to destroy them. One proposal that has been made is that as soon as bluebird young have been fledged the nests should be collected and placed in a container covered with a 12-mesh screen until adult insects have emerged from the puparia. The tiny wasps that are beneficial to bluebirds are small enough to escape through the screen, whereas the much larger blowflies would be trapped in the container and could be destroyed. This sounds good in theory, but as a practical means of controlling blowfly infestation it would not be very effective unless all bird nests within a fairly large area could be gathered up and put into screened containers at just the right time.

MITES AND LICE

Bluebirds, like most other birds, are sometimes infested with various kinds of mites (which are not true insects) and, less often, with lice. Fortunately the level of infestation is usually low enough not to be a matter for concern. At the time old nests are removed large numbers of tiny mites may be noticed both in the nesting material and running over the inside surfaces of the box. It is then a good idea to burn the nest and to treat the inside surfaces of the nesting box with a pyrethrin spray.

WASPS

Wasps—most often the so-called paper-making wasps (*Polistes* sp.) frequently find bluebird nesting boxes to their liking. Their nests, which look as though they are made of a grayish paper, consist of cells arranged in the typical honeycomb fashion, but not protected by a covering envelope. They are attached to the inner surfaces of nesting boxes by short stout stems. The most common point of attachment is the ceiling of the box.

Birds will not nest in a box inhabited by wasps, so it is important to get rid of the insects whenever they are found in a nesting box. If a wasp nest is small and only a few of the insects are in the box it can easily be removed by hand, though with care not to get stung. If more than a few wasps are present the safer course is to spray the inside of the box with a pyrethrin spray directed through the entrance hole. To be most effective this should be done in the late evening or after dark, when the entire colony of wasps will be in the box. Immediately after the spraying the entrance hole should be closed with a wad of paper or cloth. The following morning the wasp nest and dead wasps may safely be removed.

ANTS

Large numbers of ants are sometimes found in otherwise unoccupied bluebird nesting boxes, although it is hard to imagine what attracts them there. The presence of the ants may discourage bluebirds from using the box. Ants have been known to attack, kill, and devour newly hatched nestlings on occasion. They may even attack and kill the young birds by entering the eggs as soon as the shells are cracked in the hatching process.

Ants are readily killed with a pyrethrin spray. If it is necessary to spray the inside of a nesting box while the birds are nesting only one of the sprays specially formulated for use around birds should be used. If there are eggs or young birds in the nest, they should be removed carefully just before the spray is applied and then put back in the nest promptly.

The effectiveness of pyrethrins is rather short-lived. If ants persist in entering a nesting box they can usually be controlled by applying a narrow band of "Tree Tanglefoot" to the post supporting the box. This is a sticky substance commonly used in bands around the trunks of trees to control destructive crawling insects. Ants or other insects become embedded in the material when they attempt to cross it.

Two-Legged Predators

Any discussion of predators encountered on the bluebird trail would be incomplete without mentioning the common two-legged predator, *Homo sapiens*, who is sometimes the most destructive of all.

If it is discovered that the screw holding the roof or side board of a nesting box has been loosened or removed and that the nest, eggs, or nestlings not yet ready to be fledged have disappeared, the predator at work is almost certainly the two-legged kind. Sometimes nesting boxes are badly damaged by gunfire or the adult bluebirds may be found shot to death. Sometimes the exact cause of damage to a nesting box remains a mystery but the signs point to vandalism rather than natural predation. Sometimes nesting boxes simply disappear without explanation. This kind of predation is the most exasperating and inexcusable of all since the culprit is supposed to know better than to behave in this manner and he also neither needs nor uses his prey for food.

Fortunately, very few people are responsible for the problems just described. But only one or two may be enough to disrupt an entire bluebird trail. There are some steps that can be taken to minimize the likelihood of human interference. Whenever a trail is laid out along roadsides or in other public places it is a worthwhile idea to inform the community about the purpose of the project. This can be done through schools, youth organizations, social groups, and clubs. As suggested earlier, tags identifying the persons or organizations responsible for the boxes or explaining the purpose of the boxes may serve as a deterrent to some destructive impulses. The boxes can be made to blend in with their surroundings so as to be relatively inconspicuous. If the local police are informed about the bluebird trail and know the people who monitor it regularly, they may be able to help prevent unauthorized persons from tampering with the boxes, since disrupting the nests of bluebirds and most other wild birds is punishable by Federal law and the laws of most States. It is surprising how much public interest often can be aroused in a bluebird trail as the result of some well-directed public relations efforts. A standing offer to take any interested persons or groups in the community along on an inspection tour of the trail may not only reduce the chance that vandalism will take place but may win new converts to the cause of bluebird conservation.

Further Reading

Mason, E. A. 1944. Parasitism by Protocalliphora and management of cavity-nesting birds. *J. Wildlife Management* 8: 232–247.

[10]

Other Cavity-Nesting Bird Competitors

NATURALLY BLUEBIRD nesting boxes attract other kinds of cavity-nesting birds, and it is important to be able to recognize these birds and their nests and eggs. Of the various birds that may move into a well designed starling-proof bluebird box only house sparrows and, under certain circumstances, house wrens, should be unwelcome. All other species of birds that are likely to be attracted to the boxes are highly desirable and beneficial. In fact, it is a good practice to set out enough nesting boxes to meet the needs of whatever other desirable cavity-nesters happen to be in the vicinity as well as those of the bluebirds. Generally different species of birds do not mind nesting fairly close to one another. The bluebirds' sense of territorial prerogative is directed toward other bluebirds, not toward birds of other species. There is even a case on record of bluebirds and tree swallows nesting simultaneously in adjacent compartments of a two-compartment nesting box.

Identification of nests in nesting boxes may be difficult during the early stages of construction. The best way to make a positive identification at an early stage is to watch the box from a distance until one of the birds arrives with nesting material. As the nest nears completion identification on the basis of the characteristics of the nest itself becomes easier.

Starlings

Starlings will not be treated in detail here, since they are unable to enter a properly built bluebird box. It may be noted, however, that their nests are coarsely constructed of various plant materials, and that starlings ordinarily lay from 4 to 6 eggs that are a clear blue, but considerably larger than bluebird eggs.

House Sparrows

House sparrow nests are usually constructed of a wide assortment of dry plant material. If feathers are available, they are a favored sparrow building material, and they will be found especially in the linings of the nests. Unlike bluebird nests, sparrow nests are built high up along the side of the box. They are sometimes domed over at the top in such a way that the contents of the nest cannot easily be seen through the top of the box. The four to seven eggs in a house sparrow clutch are a dull white color, rather heavily speckled or splotched with olive.

As has been mentioned, house sparrow nests should be removed as often as necessary and persistence may be called for. These alien birds should never be permitted to raise their broods in bluebird boxes.

Wrens

House wrens build their nests largely of coarse twigs. They usually fill the nesting boxes almost completely, and often will partially close off the entrance holes with twigs, leaving themselves room enough to come and go but effectively denying entrance to larger competing birds. The cups of wrens' nests are lined with finer plant material and often with feathers. The five to eight eggs that are typically laid by a house wren are heavily spotted with reddish brown.

Numerous "dummy" nests consisting of twigs and all sorts of odds and ends are often built by these wrens —a habit which can make them a serious nuisance along bluebird trails. Since these "nests" are not really intended for nesting, they have little or no semblance of cups to receive eggs, and no linings.

The Carolina wren (*Thryothorus ludovicianus*) and the Bewick's wren (*Thryomanes bewickii*) also occasionally nest in bluebird boxes, but as far as is known neither of these species has the objectionable habits of the house wren. Both are delightful songsters, and both are attractive and interesting birds to have living near one's home.

Swallows

Among native birds the tree swallow (*Iridoprocne bicolor*) is the principal competitor of the bluebirds for

26. House wren nest and eggs   27. Tree swallow nest

28. Tufted titmouse nest and eggs   29. Carolina chickadee nest and eggs

nesting sites in many northern states and in most of Canada. On many bluebird trails these birds considerably outnumber the bluebirds. Tree swallows are beautiful and highly beneficial insectivorous birds. They are faced with the same general problems as the bluebirds, but to a somewhat lesser degree. Bluebirds and tree swallows seem to compete on reasonably equal terms for nesting boxes although the swallows may be slightly more aggressive. However, since bluebirds usually start nesting earlier than tree swallows they have a distinct advantage over the swallows in the choice of sites for early nesting.

Tree swallow nests are made of grass and other plant material and, unlike bluebird nests, they are almost always copiously lined with feathers. The four to six eggs (occasionally more) in a tree swallow clutch are pure white and a little smaller than bluebird eggs.

The violet-green swallow (*Tachycineta thalassina*) of the Rocky Mountain and west coast regions is an equally desirable bird. Its nesting habits, nest, and eggs are very similar to those of the tree swallow.

Chickadees

Chickadees are among the most appealing birds, and one or more of the seven closely related North American species are found in most regions of the continent. They are all cavity-nesting birds and readily accept nesting boxes that are located close to wooded areas. The species most likely to be found nesting in bluebird boxes are the Carolina chickadee (*Parus carolinensis*) of the southeastern United States, the black-capped chickadee (*Parus atricapillus*) of the northern half of the United States and most of Canada, the mountain chickadee (*Parus gambeli*) of the Rocky Mountain region, and the chestnut-backed chickadee (*Parus rufescens*) of the west coast.

Since chickadees will nest in deep woods as well as in relatively open places on the edges of woods they have not experienced the hardships that bluebirds have. They find plenty of natural cavities in woodlands where starlings and house sparrows have not yet encroached, and even where the latter two species are present chickadees can compete successfully because their small size enables them to use numerous cavities that neither starlings nor house sparrows can enter. Chickadees also have the advantage of being able to excavate their own nesting cavities if suitable natural cavities are not available.

Chickadees take great pains in building their nests and the result of their efforts is wonderful to behold. The materials used vary considerably depending on their local availability, but typically they include mosses, very fine plant fibers, and animal hairs—all of which lend themselves to the fine workmanship characteristic of a chickadee nest. Combings from the family dog are eagerly accepted by chickadees as nesting material. A neighbor once hung an expensive fur coat on her clothesline to air, but hurriedly retrieved it when my wife called to tell her that our chickadees were busily extracting hairs from the coat for their nest. In at least one instance, a chickadee was actually seen to alight on a man's head and to set about pulling out hairs for its nest!

Chickadees have rather large broods. The usual

clutch of eggs is from five to eight, or sometimes nine—and the mountain chickadee has been known to lay as many as a dozen eggs. The eggs have a dull white background and are more or less heavily spotted with light or dark reddish brown.

Anyone watching the progress of events in a chickadee nest for the first time is likely to be in for a surprise. On seeing an empty nest each day, he may wonder when the first egg will be laid. Then one day to his amazement he may find a full clutch of eight eggs where the day before there were none. Can a chickadee lay eight eggs in a single day? No, like most other birds chickadees lay but one egg each day. But as soon as each egg is laid the female chickadee carefully covers it with soft nesting material, presumably to conceal it from the eyes of any would-be predator during the egg laying period when the nest is usually left unattended. When the last egg is laid the female chickadee uncovers them all and starts incubating them.

Titmice

Titmice are slightly larger cousins of the chickadees and they all wear prominent crests. Like chickadees they often use bluebird nesting boxes located near wooded areas.

The tufted titmouse (*Parus bicolor*) has the widest geographical range of the titmice and is found throughout the eastern half of the United States except in the most northern areas.

The plain titmouse (*Parus inornatus*) is found along

the west coast north to southern Oregon and east to central Colorado and western Texas.

The black-crested titmouse (*Parus atricristatus*) is found only in south-central Texas and northeastern Mexico.

The bridled titmouse (*Parus wollweberi*) is found in the mountainous areas of southern Arizona and New Mexico and in north-central Mexico.

Titmouse nests are made from a variety of plant material, often including quantities of partially decomposed leaves, and are nearly always lined with animal hair if any is available. Like the chickadees, titmice are often so anxious to obtain sufficient hair to line their nests that they sometimes extract it from live animals. One published account tells of a tufted titmouse that cautiously approached a red squirrel from behind, then quickly and expertly extracted hair from the squirrel's tail—a move that must have involved quick reflexes since few mammals are as quick as a red squirrel. Like their cousins, the chickadees, titmice take great pains in the construction of their nests, often spending a week or more at the task. They lay from four to eight white eggs that are more or less speckled with reddish brown.

The female titmouse is most devoted to her task of incubating and protecting her eggs and young. During the incubation period of roughly twelve days she leaves the nest infrequently and only for short periods. Much of her food is supplied by her mate while she remains on the nest. If a nesting box is opened while the female titmouse is incubating her eggs she frequently assumes a threatening posture, uttering vicious snake-like hissing sounds in a brave effort to frighten the intruder away.

Nuthatches

Nuthatches are the familiar little bluish gray-backed acrobats of the bird world that run along tree branches and either up or down the trunks with equal facility—always headfirst. One or more of the four North American species may be found almost everywhere in the United States except in a rather narrow north-south corridor through the Great Plains.

The white-breasted nuthatch (*Sitta carolinensis*) is widely distributed throughout most of the country and is the species most commonly seen near human habitations as well as in the wilds. It is the largest of the four species.

The red-breasted nuthatch (*Sitta canadensis*) breeds in Canada and in the northern parts of the northern United States, as well as much farther south in the Rocky Mountain and Appalachian regions.

The brown-headed nuthatch (*Sitta pusilla*) has a rather limited range in the southeastern part of the country.

The pygmy nuthatch (*Sitta pygmaea*) is found throughout the Rocky Mountain region from southern Canada to southern Mexico. It is very similar to the brown-headed nuthatch but has a grayer cap.

All nuthatches are cavity-nesting birds and all may use bluebird nesting boxes from time to time, especially if the boxes are close to wooded areas. White-breasted nuthatches are the ones most likely to nest in nesting boxes. The three smaller species seem to prefer to excavate their own cavities in partially decayed dead trees.

All of the nuthatches will accept ready-made nesting sites where there is a shortage of dead trees or branches, however. A pair of brown-headed nuthatches recently nested and raised a brood of six in a nesting box only forty feet from the home of good friends of mine in North Carolina. This was actually quite unusual, since this species does not commonly use artificial nesting sites, nor does it usually nest so close to human habitations.

Nuthatches use quite a variety of nesting materials but shreds of bark are the most common material used for the body of the nest. The nest may then be lined with fine grasses, feathers, or animal hair. Rabbit fur, when it is available, seems to be a favorite nest lining material for all nuthatches.

All nuthatch eggs are white, more or less heavily speckled with reddish brown. The clutch normally consists of from five to eight eggs.

Woodpeckers

All woodpeckers are cavity-nesting birds. They usually excavate their own cavities in dead trees, but occasionally some of them will use nesting boxes. Bluebird nesting boxes are too small to accommodate any of the woodpeckers comfortably with the exception of the downy woodpecker. This delightful little bird, the smallest North American representative of the woodpecker family, is widely distributed over most of the United States and Canada.

Like all woodpeckers, the downy woodpecker builds no nest at all but lays its eggs on the accumulation of small chips of wood and other material usually found at the bottom of natural cavities. Woodpeckers are more likely to use a nesting box if the floor of the box is covered with about an inch of small wood chips or a mixture of coarse sawdust and soil.

A friend of mine told me the interesting tale of a flicker that had taken a fancy to one of her bluebird boxes and set about remodeling it to suit his own needs. Since the entrance hole was much too small for this large woodpecker to enter, he worked long and hard with his powerful bill to enlarge it. Having accomplished that, he entered the box and evidently decided it was too small, and particularly not deep enough, so he set about remedying that as well. After many hours of hard work he was startled to find that he had broken through the bottom of the box to the outside world. Realizing that his cherished new home was no longer fit to hold his mate's eggs, he gave up the project in evident disgust.

Flickers readily accept nesting boxes built to the right specifications for them. The entrance hole should be 2½" in diameter and about 15" above the floor. The floor dimensions should be about 7" x 7". Flicker boxes should never be set out anywhere where starlings are common, since the starlings will inevitably usurp them.

Flycatchers

Among the flycatchers only those of the genus *Myiarchus*, the crested flycatchers, are cavity nesters and potential occupants of nesting boxes. The great crested flycatcher (*Myiarchus crinitus*) breeds throughout the eastern half of the United States. The ash-throated fly-catcher (*Myiarchus cinerascens*) is rather widely distrib-uted in the southwestern third of the country and up the west coast as far as the state of Washington. The oliva-ceous flycatcher (*Myiarchus tuberculifer*) and the Wied's crested flycatcher (*Myiarchus tyrannulus*) are both found only in the extreme southwestern part of the country and in Mexico.

Great crested flycatchers in particular, like the blue-birds, have suffered badly as a result of encroachment by starlings in recent years. They have been driven from most areas close to human habitations where they for-merly nested freely. Two recent reports of great crested flycatchers nesting in nesting boxes on bluebird trails were investigated carefully because it has generally been assumed that these birds were unable to enter the $1\frac{1}{2}''$ entrance holes of bluebird nesting boxes. In both cases it was found that the entrance holes were $1\frac{9}{16}''$, just $\frac{1}{16}''$ larger than that recommended for bluebirds and a mere $\frac{1}{16}''$ smaller than the minimum size that will admit star-lings. If additional studies should confirm these prelim-inary findings it would be an important development, for a way would be opened to entice these lovely flycatchers back to suburban gardens where their haunting calls gave so many people pleasure through the years before the advent of the starlings.

If a nesting box is being specially made for great crested flycatchers the plans given in this book for blue-bird boxes may be followed. But the floor of the box should be at least $5'' \times 5''$ to accommodate the flycatchers, since they are larger than bluebirds and also tend to have larger broods. Where starlings are around, the entrance hole should be exactly 1⁹⁄₁₆″ in diameter, as it was in the two bluebird boxes in which the flycatchers were recently reported to be nesting. In areas where there are no starlings a somewhat larger entrance (up to 2″ in diameter) might be better. The boxes are most likely to attract flycatchers if they are located close to wooded areas and in among scattered trees.

The great crested flycatcher has the strange habit of incorporating into its nest a large piece of snakeskin if one can be found. If there is no snakeskin to be had, a piece of thin plastic wrapping may be pressed to service instead. The function of the snakeskin is unknown. but one theory is that it is introduced into the nest in an attempt to frighten away predators. Whatever the reason for using it, and whatever its effect may be on other predators, I can attest to the fact that starlings are totally unimpressed by the snakeskin when they decide to evict flycatchers from a cavity or nesting box.

The ash-throated flycatcher of the west is slightly smaller than the great crested flycatcher. It can readily enter the 1½″ opening in bluebird nesting boxes, and will actually use these boxes for nesting. The same is no doubt true for the still smaller olivaceous flycatcher.

Further Reading

Hersey, F. S. 1933. Notes on Tree Swallows and Bluebirds. *Auk* 50: 109–110.

Reed, C. E. 1924. Bluebirds, swallows, and wrens. *Bird-Lore* 26: 116–117.

[11]
Bluebird
Foster
Children

As I STARTED to write this account on an early September day a beautiful 33-day-old eastern bluebird (*Sialia sialis*) alighted gently on my shoulder from a nearby tree. He warbled sweetly but insistently in my ear, telling me in unmistakable bluebird language that it was time to eat even though he had just gorged himself a half hour earlier. Soon he was joined by his equally beautiful and hungry brother and sister and the three of them made such a clamor that I had to lay down my work and stuff the three gaping mouths with an unnatural but well balanced bluebird diet mixture from our kitchen. These charming adopted orphans always lingered a minute or so after eating, expressing their satisfaction with soft murmuring sounds seldom heard by man. Then they would fly out of sight to explore more of their new world only to return ravenous in another thirty minutes or so. They were wild and free, but not yet sufficiently experienced to find more than a small part of their own food.

It all began on the early morning of August 14 when I was monitoring the few remaining late broods on my bluebird trail near Beltsville, Maryland. I knew that my nesting box No. 325 should contain four ten-day-old nestlings, nearly the last of the 193 young bluebirds fledged on the Beltsville trail during the season. On opening the box I was dismayed to find that the nestlings appeared to be dead. I removed the nest and on closer examination found that three of the nestlings showed the faintest perceptible signs of life, but the fourth was unquestionably dead. The three live nestlings were limp, almost motionless, and completely cold, no warmer to the touch than their dead sibling. It seemed probable that the parent birds had somehow both been killed and that the nestlings had not eaten for twenty hours or more. Had only one parent perished the survivor would have cared for the baby birds.

My first impulse was to discard the brood and proceed with my monitoring since the nestlings seemed to be beyond any reasonable hope. This I probably would have done if they were anything but bluebirds. But baby bluebirds are too precious to abandon if there is even the faintest hope of saving them. So I opened my shirt, held the cold babies against my body to warm them, and drove with one hand over the nine miles to my home. By the time I arrived, the birds were warmer and were beginning to move. They were still too weak to utter a sound or to open their mouths, so my wife and I force-fed them every few minutes with tiny pieces of raw beef, gently pressing the food deep into their throats until their reflexes forced them to swallow. Within an hour they had regained enough strength to open their mouths feebly for food and to chirp very faintly. By the end of the day they were alert, strong, very vocal, and were clamoring for food almost incessantly. To me their recovery was a miracle.

Now that we had saved these charming wild baby birds from certain death we were morally committed to serve as their foster parents and thereby to accept the responsibility for their safe and proper upbringing. So we kept them in a crude nest made of facial tissue in a small open box, and about every twenty minutes from dawn to dusk we fed them and removed the fecal sacs as all good bluebird parents do. We whistled before offering them food so that they would learn to associate our whistle with feeding time, an important lesson for them later when they were released. The amount of food they consumed and their rate of growth seemed incredible. During this period we felt free to go where we wished as we could easily take the birds with us. They were fed frequently en route on one 150-mile trip.

When the birds were nineteen days old, about the normal fledging age, they scrambled to the top of their box, stretched their wings, and were ready for their maiden flights. Rather than release them then, however, we transferred them to a small flight cage where they could practice flying and where we could teach them an unnatural but all-important lesson made necessary by our human inadequacy as bluebird foster parents. We knew that when young bluebirds first fly they instinctively take to the tall trees and remain there for days in relative safety from most predators. When hungry they call for food which the parents promptly supply. We knew that without special training our fledgling bluebirds would expect us to deliver their food to the treetops as all good bluebird parents do. Since this was a service we were physically incapable of supplying we considered it necessary to spend two arduous days teaching our young birds to come to us for food. Although stubborn at first, they learned their lesson rapidly as do nearly all living creatures when failure to learn means the threat of starvation.

The young bluebirds were released at the age of twenty-one days. They flew remarkably well and reveled in their freedom, but returned to us every half hour or so for food. They had learned their lesson well. By the time they were five weeks old they were full grown, well developed, and incredibly beautiful; more beautiful, we thought, than their counterparts reared by natural parents. (Parental pride, no doubt!) The young birds stayed close together at all times and were often seen huddled tightly together on a branch, particularly when it rained. They responded to our whistle when they were out of sight and they called insistently to us near our back door if we did not appear with food at the proper time. If we still failed to appear they would fly from window to window, peering in until they located one of us. They aroused us at dawn by clamoring at our bedroom window. Impatient for their breakfast, they pestered me at the bathroom window while I shaved. They would alight without fear on our heads, shoulders, or outstretched hands to be fed, and often remained there long after they had eaten, warbling softly or pecking at us ever so gently as though caressing us. Sometimes

30. Orphaned bluebirds, age 15 days   31. Orphaned bluebird, age 33 days

32. Orphaned bluebirds, male and female, age 89 days

they would even cuddle up under our chins for short naps when their stomachs were full. To them, *we* were their parents and it was easy to imagine that they had the same affection for us that we had for them.

At the age of six weeks the young birds were mature and agile enough to obtain their own food but like most youngsters preferred the easy way of having it given to them. So again we did our best to emulate parent blue-birds by gradually reducing the amount and frequency of feedings. This weaning process seemed cruel and heartless, but again hunger speeded the learning process and the young birds soon became adept at catching juicy insects, nature's bluebird food. At last we seemed to have accomplished our goal of raising these babies to a self-sufficient and completely independent adulthood. Our hope and expectation was that they would find and travel with others of their kind, that they would live and behave like normal bluebirds, and that they would for-get their strange upbringing and learn to regard man in his proper light as one of their natural enemies.

Our aspirations for our foster children, however, were not to be realized so easily, and we soon found that we were destined to play further fascinating roles in their remarkable lives. After all, in their eyes we were still their real parents and bluebirds have strong family ties. Although they roamed over considerable distances they continued steadfastly to be part of our family, perhaps since there were no others of their kind within miles with which they could associate. In their memory they had never seen other bluebirds. They no longer needed us for any material support, yet they continued to come to us daily for an occasional choice snack from our hands, but often for no apparent reason other than to carry on a little friendly conversation to which they contributed their full share. Perhaps to them this satisfied an emotional need since they had no natural parents, and to us this continued confidence and seeming affection for us was a source of great emotional satisfaction.

In autumn our young birds gradually lost their juvenile plumage and blossomed out into their gorgeous adult coats. They remained with us throughout the winter living mainly on wild berries, but they continued to come to our hands daily for small handouts. One of the two male birds finally fell prey to a neighborhood cat much to our sorrow, although we had long feared such an event.

With the approach of spring our two remaining orphans became increasingly restless and wandered farther and farther from home. The mating season was at hand and we suspected that they might be searching for mates other than each other and for a more suitable bluebird habitat for nesting. If this were so their search was a failure, and not surprisingly so, since no other bluebirds had inhabited our area for many years. So they soon ceased their wanderings and remained almost constantly at home.

It soon became apparent that the orphaned male had never before fully appreciated the female's charms. But now at last he realized how beautiful and lovely she really was. He brought her the choicest insects he could find which she accepted graciously with wings aflutter. He had never had an opportunity to learn the traditional song of the bluebird, so he composed his own love songs and sang them to her with passionate tenderness.* He selected one of the old nesting boxes mounted on a metal post in our garden and with unrestrained enthusiasm urged her to accept it and by so doing to accept him as her mate. After some hesitation she indicated her acceptance by carrying a bit of dry grass into the box. This simple symbolic act of hers aroused the male to the wildest imaginable exhibition of joy. He flew in wavering circles around their new home while his normally soft singing rose in a great crescendo of uninhibited ecstasy.

The honeymoon was soon over and hard work lay ahead. The female worked long hours selecting suitable grasses and fashioning them into a cozy nest, exactly as her mother and female ancestors for countless generations had done. She then laid a beautiful blue egg in her nest each morning for four days. After this was done she sat faithfully on her eggs for fourteen days to keep them warm, leaving the nest only for short periods to obtain food. During all this time her mate supported her morale by singing softly to her from a nearby perch, by bringing her an occasional succulent insect, and by savagely driving away any other bird that had the temerity to show interest in their nesting box.

The eggs all hatched on schedule on the fourteenth day of incubation. Both parents then worked tirelessly

* Carefully controlled studies at Cornell University (Allen [1962]) demonstrated that all of the ordinary call notes of the bluebird are inherited, but that the true song of the species is learned only through imitation.

bringing insects every few minutes from dawn to dusk to feed the rapidly growing baby birds. In seventeen days the babies were ready to fly. They flew successfully from their nesting box to nearby low bushes and trees from which they gradually worked their way up to the treetops. Two of them were lost to unknown predators on the first day out of the nest; but the other two, both males, survived this most crucial period in the lives of all songbirds. These two remained high in the trees for about a week, spending much of their time flying from tree to tree to gain strength and flying skill. The parent birds knew where they were at all times and furnished them with an endless supply of insects.

When the youngsters were twenty-four days old they descended to lower levels and began to inspect the ground from which they eventually would have to learn to obtain most of their own food. At this time, and much to our amazement, the parent birds brought their two babies to our back door and quite obviously encouraged them to accept food from our hands. Naturally we were pleased and flattered by this additional display of confidence. We wondered if we were now to become foster grandparents to a new generation of bluebirds.

Within a few days the female parent turned over the entire care of the twins to her mate, who in turn continued to solicit our help. The female had more important work to do. She immediately set about building a new nest, laying another set of eggs, and raising a second brood.

Tragedy struck again when the new brood was eight days old. The mother bird appeared at our door on that

33. The author is paid a visit by two
of his bluebird friends

(Photo by Dickson Preston)

morning obviously quite ill. She was unable to accept
her customary breakfast, but flew rather feebly back
toward her nest. She was not seen again all day. The
next morning my wife, fearful that some misfortune
might have occurred, stood in the garden watching the
nesting box. The male was busy bringing food to the
tiny nestlings but there was no sign of his mate. Finally
he brought a light blue feather out of the nesting box
and with a long meaningful look gently laid it on a post
directly in front of my wife's face and within a foot of
where she was standing. Her suspicion was fully aroused
when within a minute or two he repeated this perform-
ance. So we climbed up and unscrewed the top of the
nesting box. To our great sorrow we found the body of
the female bluebird where she had gone to die beside
her beloved new babies.

Had her mate been trying to tell us something?
Surely he had desperately needed help to remove his

mate's dead body from the nesting box where the baby birds would need to remain for another ten days. And just as surely he communicated this message effectively to one of his human foster parents. Did he do this by deliberate intent or by accident? No one can say for sure.

Undaunted, the widowed male assumed full responsibility for the care and feeding of the new brood. On the following day the two older fledglings, who had only recently learned to find their own food, likewise rose to the emergency and bravely helped in feeding the rapidly growing new babies. The combined efforts of these three male birds were fully repaid when the three new young, one male and two females, left their nest on schedule and survived the hazardous period when they learned to fly and later to take care of all of their own needs.

The birds continued to come to us regularly for a small part of their food supply. But none of the new generation looked upon us as their parents. To them we were simply an easy source of food which they would snatch quickly and then fly off. They showed no recognition of our whistle and they had no inclination to remain perched on our hands or to carry on any "conversation" or other intimacies with us as their parents had always done. The beautiful and delicate rapport that we had established with our original "foster children" was totally lacking in the second generation. This we considered to be quite proper and understandable as the new youngsters had a real father and two older brothers to support them, and furthermore we had no desire to domesticate these wild birds.

In the early autumn our bluebird family began to wander and we never knew from day to day when or if we might see them again. Finally they were gone. We believe that they fulfilled their instinctive desire to join with other bluebird families into a small flock which would spend the winter months in some sheltered area where wild berries are abundant, and that they would perhaps move farther south if the winter should be severe. We also believe that we fulfilled *our* desire to save a small family of bluebird orphans and return them to the wild where they would help propagate this lovely but disappearing species, even though two generations were required to accomplish our goal.

No one should attempt to hand raise young wild birds unless it is certain that they are orphaned or abandoned.* Too often well-meaning people unwittingly kidnap young birds in the mistaken belief that they are not being cared for. But in cases where nestlings can be saved from certain death, their temporary adoption is justified and can be a most rewarding experience. One gains an insight into wild bird nature that can be obtained in no other way.

In the case of our orphaned bluebirds there can be no doubt that limited two-way vocal communication was

---

* A Federal permit is required to hand raise any native wild bird. Application for such a permit may be made to the nearest District Office of the U.S. Fish and Wildlife Service, Law Enforcement Division, U.S. Department of the Interior.

established which was clearly understood by both bird and man. There was also strong evidence of mutual affection, but this, of course, would be difficult to prove. One who has had an experience like ours, however, may find it difficult to accept the prevailing belief that all bird behavior is guided by instinct alone.

Further Reading

Price, J. 1975. Bluebird on my shoulder. *Virginia Wildlife* 36 (7): 18–20.

THE FEEDING OF ORPHANED BLUEBIRDS

Bluebird nestlings that are at least a week old and that have been orphaned or abandoned can usually be hand-raised successfully. (But see the footnote on page 155.) The nestlings should be fed approximately every twenty minutes from dawn to dusk in order to simulate as nearly as possible the natural feeding schedule for individual nestlings. When the young birds are about eighteen days old they should be taught to come to the person offering them food at each feeding time. The birds should be released when they are about twenty days old. Feeding must then be continued for about three more weeks until the young birds are able to obtain their own food.

Insects such as caterpillars and moths are the best foods to use, since they are among the principal items in the nestlings' natural diet. Meal worms are excellent and can be obtained at most pet stores. A good grade of canned dog food is also satisfactory, particularly the kind specially formulated for puppies and sold by most veterinarians. Lean ground beef may be used, but a small amount of dibasic calcium phosphate with vitamin D (obtainable at most drug stores) should be mixed with it. Small pieces of hard-boiled egg yolk, raw liver, and raisins are excellent supplementary foods. Do not give young bluebirds water or other liquids until they are able to drink by themselves. The food given them usually contains enough water for their requirements, although it is all right to dip an occasional piece of their food in water momentarily before it is eaten.

[12]
Bluebirds
for the
Future

No ONE who has read up to this point will fail to see wny bluebirds are now in need of help. The time for action is now at hand. If we wait until only a few hundreds or a few thousands of the birds survive—as has been the case with some of our other threatened species of wildlife—the chances of saving them will be slight. But hundreds of individuals and organizations across North America have already rallied to the cause of bluebird conservation, and if enough others join them there is every reason to be confident that within the lifetime of most of those reading this book bluebirds could be restored to their former numbers and assured a place in the future of this globe. In fact, data on the eastern bluebird included in the large-scale "Breeding Bird Surveys" (Robbins and Van Velzen [1967]) that have been conducted by the U.S. Fish and Wildlife Service since 1966 justify some cautious optimism. Although a steady decline in the eastern bluebird population occurred during the period 1966–69, each of the subsequent years through 1972 showed some recovery. The recovery continued in 1973 east of the Appalachians, but was reversed in the eastern portions of the Mississippi Valley—probably as a result of severe freezing rains in large parts of that region during the previous winter (Robbins [1974]). Preliminary data indicate a continuing decline in the population of the western bluebird but no significant change for the mountain bluebird during the short period of the survey.

I should like to think that the recent upturn in the eastern bluebird population is attributable in some part at least to increased public awareness of the bluebirds' plight and the establishment of new bluebird trails and expansion of older trails since 1969. But it should also be noted that with the exception noted above (1973) relatively mild winters occurred in the south throughout the period of the recovery. One or two severe winters in the southern part of the country could quickly erase the recent gains and could even reduce the population of the eastern bluebird to new low levels. Only widespread public participation in bluebird conservation efforts along the lines suggested in this book can decisively alter the bluebirds' long-range prospects for survival.

Bluebird conservation offers an unusual opportunity for people who are truly concerned about our wildlife heritage to accomplish something by means of direct action. Although public concern over the disappearance of wildlife has greatly increased in recent years, in most cases those who are concerned can do little more than support favorable legislation and contribute money to organizations that are battling for the preservation of wildlife. But thousands of these concerned people long for an opportunity to do something tangible, to become personally involved in an activity that will help save some valuable species of wildlife from annihilation. Bluebird conservation is ideally suited to this purpose because almost anyone can participate in it and see with his—or her—own eyes the results of his efforts. Access to rural or semi-rural property is necessary, but access is often more easily obtained than one might suppose for the establishment of a bluebird trail, once the purpose of the trail has been explained.

I receive innumerable letters from people in all walks of life—working people, retired people, city people, and country people—expressing in glowing terms the joy and satisfaction that they have obtained from watching the courtship and family lives of bluebirds they have attracted by providing the nesting boxes described in this book. The lives of these people are enriched by the realization that they are doing something tangible to help a lovely form of life survive. The same satisfaction can be yours. Bluebird conservation is a task that cannot be accomplished by law, edict, oratory, or armchair philosophy. It can be accomplished only through broad and active public participation. The cost is small but the reward is great. Please help if you can. The "bluebird of happiness" may then come to *you!*

BIBLIOGRAPHY

Allen, A. A. 1962. Sapsucker Woods, Cornell's exciting new bird sanctuary. *National Geographic* 121: 530–551.

Anonymous. 1967. Bluebird populations and nestboxes. *Atlantic Naturalist* 22: 26–31.

Atkinson, B. 1974. Fewer bluebirds are heralding spring's return. *Smithsonian* 5 (1): 38–45.

Beal, F. E. 1915. *Food of the Robins and Bluebirds of the United States.* U. S. Dept. Agr., Dept. Bull. 171.

Bell, R. K. 1968. A bird bander's diary. *Eastern Bird Banding Assn. News* 31: 63–66.

————. 1971. A bird bander's diary, *EBBA News* 34: 127–129.

Bent, A. C. 1949. *Life Histories of North American Thrushes, Kinglets, and their Allies.* U. S. Natl. Mus. Bull. 196: 233–288.

Blake, C. H. 1954. Death of a Bluebird. *Bird-Banding* 25: 59.

Broderick, H. J. 1938. Nesting and re-mating of a pair of bluebirds. *Auk* 55: 538–539.

Burroughs, J. 1871. The Bluebird. *The Writings of John Burroughs* 1: 205–216.

Carr, T. and Gain, C. J., Jr. 1965. Bluebirds feeding Mockingbird nestlings. *Wilson Bull.* 77: 405–406.

Chapman, F. M. 1924. *Handbook of Birds of Eastern North America.* D. Appleton & Co., p. 356.

Clark, J. 1904. A plea for bird-boxes. *Bird-Lore* 6: 66.

Criddle, N. 1927. Habits of the mountain bluebirds in Manitoba. *Canadian Field Naturalist* 41: 40–44.

Davidson, V. E. 1962. What bluebirds eat. *Audubon Magazine* 64: 223–224.

Dobroscky, I. D. 1925. External parasites of birds and the fauna of birds' nests. *Biol. Bull.* 48: 274–281.

Draper, G. S. 1971. Eleven days with the bluebirds. *Wildlife in North Carolina*, Aug. 1971: 8–10.

Fast, A. H. 1955. Bluebirds attracted by peanut hearts. *Bird-Banding* 26: 27–28.

Finch, J. R. 1972. *Disappearance of the Eastern Bluebird in Tobacco Producing Areas*. (Report distributed by the author. Address: Route 1, Bailey, N. C. 27807).

Frazier, A. and Nolan, V., Jr. 1959. Communal roosting by the Eastern Bluebird in winter. *Bird-Banding* 30: 219–226.

Friedmann, H. 1934. Further additions to the list of birds victimized by the Cowbird. *Wilson Bull.* 46: 25–26.

Gannon, R. 1962. To bring back the bluebird. *Reader's Digest*, March 1962: 231–236.

Gardner, A. F. 1920. Bluebirds vs. Wrens. *Bird-Lore* 22: 163–164.

Grand Rapids Audubon Club. 1974. *Bluebirds and Martins Unlimited*. New edition published annually by the Club, 54 Jefferson Ave., S. E., Grand Rapids, Mich. 49502. Price: 25¢.

Grange, W. B. and McAtee, W. L. 1942. *Improving the Farm Environment for Wildlife*. U. S. Dept. Int., Fish and Wildlife Serv. Conservation Bull. 12.

Hamilton, W., Jr. 1943. Nesting of the Eastern Bluebird. *Auk* 60: 91–94.

Harper, W. T. 1926. A Bluebird's nest. *Bird-Lore* 28: 187–190.

Hartshorne, J. M. 1962. Behavior of the Eastern Bluebird at the nest. *The Living Bird* I: 131–149.

Hersey, F. S. 1933. Notes on Tree Swallows and Bluebirds. *Auk* 50: 109–110.

Highhouse, W. L. 1964. "Operation Bluebird" in Warren County, Pennsylvania. Eighth report. *Kingbird* 14: 210–212.

Hodge, C. T. 1904. A summer with bluebirds. *Bird-Lore* 6: 41–46.

James, D. 1961–63. The changing seasons. *Audubon Field Notes* 15: 304–308; 16: 308–311; 17: 300–304.

Johnson, C. W. 1932. Notes on Protocalliphora during the summer of 1931. *Bird-Banding* 3: 26–29.

Kelly, M. 1968. Birdhouses for Bluebirds and other desirable species. *Conservationist* 22: 47–48.

Kibler, L. F. 1969. The establishment and maintenance of a bluebird nest-box project. A review and commentary. *Bird-Banding* 40: 114–129.

Krieg, D. C. 1962. Bluebird nest box project. *Kingbird* 14: 26–27.

_____. 1971. *The Behavioral Patterns of the Eastern Bluebird.* N. Y. State Museum and Science Service, Bull. No. 415.

Lane, J. 1968. A hybrid Eastern Bluebird x Mountain Bluebird. *Auk* 85: 684.

_____. 1969. Hybridism in the Eastern and Mountain Bluebirds. *The Blue Jay* 27: 18–21.

_____. 1971. Eleventh annual nestbox report of the Brandon Junior Birders. *The Blue Jay* 29: 209.

_____. 1972. Twelfth annual nestbox report of the Brandon Junior Birders. *The Blue Jay* 30: 226–227.

_____, and Martin, C. 1973. Thirteenth annual nestbox report. *The Blue Jay* 31: 235–236.

Laskey, A. R. 1939. A study of nesting Eastern Bluebirds. *Bird-Banding* 10: 23–32.

_____. 1940. The 1939 nesting season of bluebirds at Nashville, Tennessee. Wilson Bull. 52: 183–190.

_____. 1943. The nesting of Bluebirds banded as nestlings. *Bird-Banding* 14: 39–43.

_____. 1946. Snake depredations at bird nests. *Wilson Bull.* 58: 217–218.

_____. 1956. The bluebird nest-box project at Nashville, Tennessee. *Inland Bird Banding News* 28: 29–30.

_____, and Herbert, M. F. 1968. Nesting of bluebirds at Ashland City. *The Migrant* 39: 73–74.

_____. 1969. Eastern Bluebird nesting in 1969 at Ashland City. *The Migrant* 40: 81–82.

_____. 1971. Eastern Bluebird nesting at Ashland City, 1970. *The Migrant* 42: 14–15.

_____. 1972. Eastern Bluebird nesting at Ashland City: 1971. *The Migrant* 43: 65–66.

Ligon, J. D. 1969. Factors influencing breeding range expansion of the Azure Bluebird. *Wilson Bull.* 81: 104–105.

Lincoln, F. C. 1950. *Migration of Birds.* U. S. Dept. Int., Fish and Wildlife Serv., Circ. 16.

Lindstrom, A. 1973. Happiness is a bluebird trail. *NRTA Journal* 24, May-June: 64–65.

Low, S. H. 1933. Notes on the nesting of Bluebirds. *Bird-Banding* 4: 109–111.

————. 1934. Bluebird studies at Cape Cod. *Bird-Banding* 5: 39–41.

McAtee, W. L. 1947 (rev.). *Attracting Birds*. U. S. Dept. Int., Fish and Wildlife Serv. Conservation Bull. 1.

McKnight, E. T. 1973. A nest box project for bluebirds in Stafford County, Virginia. *The Raven* 44: 59–68.

Mason, E. A. 1944. Parasitism by Protocalliphora and management of cavity-nesting birds. *J. Wildlife Management* 8: 232–247.

Miller, W. 1970. Factors influencing the status of Eastern and Mountain Bluebirds in southwestern Manitoba. *The Blue Jay* 28: 38–46.

Musselman, T. E. 1934. Help the bluebirds. *Bird-Lore* 36: 9–13.

————. 1935. Three years of Eastern Bluebird banding and study. *Bird-Banding* 6: 117–125.

————. 1939. The effect of cold snaps upon the nesting of the Eastern Bluebird. *Bird-Banding* 10: 33–35.

National Association of Audubon Societies. n.d. *Golf Clubs as Bird Sanctuaries*.

Peakall, D. B. 1970. The Eastern Bluebird: its breeding season, clutch size, and nesting success. *The Living Bird* IX: 239–256.

Peters, H. S. 1930. Ectoparasites and bird-banding. *Bird-Banding* 1: 51–60.

Peterson, R. T. 1947. *A Field Guide to the Birds*. Boston: Houghton Mifflin Co.

————. 1961. *A Field Guide to Western Birds*. Boston: Houghton Mifflin Co.

Pettingill, O. S. 1936. Breeding behavior of Bluebirds. *Auk* 53: 86–87.

Pinkowski, B. C. 1971a. Some observations on the vocalizations of the Eastern Bluebird. *Bird-Banding* 42: 20–27.

————. 1971b. An analysis of banding-recovery data on Eastern Bluebirds banded in Michigan and three neighboring States. *The Jack-Pine Warbler* 49: 33–50.

————. 1974a. Prolonged incubation record for an Eastern Bluebird. *Inland Bird Banding News* 46: 15–20.

————. 1974b. Criteria for sexing Eastern Bluebirds in juvenile plumage. *Inland Bird Banding News* 46: 88–91.

————. 1974c. The Eastern Bluebird pair bond: Comments and calculations. *EBBA News* 37: 107–110.

————. 1975a. *A Comparative Study of the Behavioral and Breeding Ecology of the Eastern Bluebird (Sialia sialis)*. Ph.D. dissertation, 471 pp., published on demand by Xerox University Microfilms, P.O. Box 1346, Ann Arbor, Mich. 48106.

————. 1975b. Yearling male Eastern Bluebird assists parents in feeding young. *Auk* 92: 801–802.

————. 1975c. A summary and key for determining causes of nesting failures in Eastern Bluebirds using nesting boxes. *Inland Bird Banding News* 47: 179–186.

Potter, R. P. 1967. Rotenone for bird houses. *Eastern Birdbanding Assn. News* 30: 88–89.

Power, H. W. 1975. Mountain Bluebirds: Experimental evidence against altruism. *Science* 189: 142–143.

Power, H. W. III. 1966. Biology of the Mountain Bluebird in Montana. *Condor* 68: 351–371.

Prescott, H. 1975. June cold takes Oregon bluebird toll. *Purple Martin News* 10 (7): 9.

Preston, F. W. and McCormick, J. M. 1948. The eyesight of the bluebird. *Wilson Bull.* 60: 120.

Price, J. 1975. Bluebird on my shoulder. *Virginia Wildlife* 36 (7): 18–20.

Reed, C. E. 1924. Bluebirds, swallows, and wrens. *Bird-Lore* 26: 116–117.

Robbins, C. S.; Brunn, B.; Zim, H. S.; and Singer, A. 1966. *Birds of North America*. New York: Golden Press.

Robbins, C. S. 1974. Monitoring bird population trends. *Timber-Wildlife Management Symposium*. Missouri Academy of Science, pp. 96–100. Occasional Paper 3.

———— and Van Velzen, W. T. 1967. *The Breeding Bird Survey, 1966*. U. S. Dept. Int., Fish and Wildlife Serv., Special Scientific Report—Wildlife No. 102.

Romig, M. & Mrs. P. W. n.d. *Bluebird Trails Guide*. Wisconsin Society for Ornithology, Bull. 137.

Sawyer, E. J. 1969. *Homes for Wildlife.* Cranbrook Institute of Science, Bull. 1, 6th ed.

Schreiber, E. D. 1938. Bluebird "Better Housing" project. *The Migrant,* March 1938: 4–6.

Scott, L. 1970. Annual report of the Indian Head bluebird trail. *The Blue Jay* 28: 176–177.

──────. 1971. Annual report of the Indian Head bluebird trail project. *The Blue Jay* 29: 209–210.

──────. 1972. Annual report of the Indian Head bluebird trail. *The Blue Jay* 30: 227.

──────. 1973. A report from the Indian Head trails. *Purple Martin Capital News* 8 (7): 4.

Sister Barbara Ann. 1970. Five years' experience with a bluebird population. *Maryland Birdlife* 26: 81–92.

Smith, W. P. 1937. Some bluebird observations. *Bird-Banding* 8: 25–30.

Summers-Smith, J. D. 1963. *The House Sparrow.* London: Collins, p. 176.

Terres, J. K. 1968. *Songbirds in Your Garden.* New York: Thomas Y. Crowell Co. Chapter 10.

Thomas, J. W., Brush, R. O., and DeGraff, R. M. 1973. Invite wildlife to your backyard. *National Wildlife* 11 (3): 5–16.

Thomas, R. H. 1946. A study of Eastern Bluebirds in Arkansas. *Wilson Bull.* 58: 143–183.

U. S. Department of Agriculture. 1969. *Invite Birds to Your Home.* Soil Cons. Serv. PA-940.

U. S. Department of the Interior. 1969 (rev.). *Homes for Birds.* Fish and Wildlife Serv., Conservation Bull. 14.

Varner, D. A. 1964. How to make a sparrow-free Bluebird box route. *Inland Bird-Banding News* 36: 93–95.

Watson, G. E. and Amerson, A. B., Jr. 1967. *Instructions for Collecting Bird Parasites.* Smithsonian Institution, Museum of Natural History Information Leaflet 477.

Weatherbee, K. B. 1933. Eastern Bluebirds in juvenal plumage feed young of second brood. *Bird-Banding* 4: 199–200.

Webster, C. G. and Uhler, F. M. 1964 (slightly revised 1966). *Improved Nest Structures for Wood Ducks.* U. S. Dept. Int. Wildlife Leaflet 458.

White, S. C. and Woolfenden, G. E. 1973. Breeding of the Eastern Bluebird in central Florida. *Bird-Banding* 44: 110–123.

Whiting, A. R. 1967. The biology of the parasitic wasp, *Mormoniella vitripennis Nasonia brevicornis* (Walker). *Quarterly Review of Biology* 42: 333–406.

Woodward, P. W. 1973. An easily made bluebird house. *Maryland Birdlife* 29: 151–152.

Zeleny, L. 1967. Bluebird nest box project—1967 report. *Atlantic Naturalist* 22: 224–226.

————. 1968a. *Bluebirds for Posterity*. National Assn. for the Protection and Propagation of the Purple Martins and Bluebirds of America.

————. 1968b. Bluebird nesting box temperatures. *Atlantic Naturalist* 23: 214–218.

————. 1969a. Starlings versus native cavity-nesting birds. *Atlantic Naturalist* 24: 158–161.

————. 1969b. The M.O.S. bluebird project. *Maryland Birdlife* 25: 138–142.

————. 1970. Unusual bluebird behavior in the care of nestlings. *Maryland Birdlife* 26: 93–95.

————. 1971a. About bluebird courtship. *Purple Martin Capital News* 6 (2): 6.

————. 1971b. The Beltsville bluebird trail. *Purple Martin Capital News* 6 (3): 31.

————. 1972. Can we save the bluebird? *The Living Wilderness* 36 (119): 24–31.

————. 1973a. Help the bluebird. *National Parks and Conservation Magazine* 47 (4): 13–17.

————. 1973b. Bluebird nesting box project 1973. *Atlantic Naturalist* 28: 155–158.

————. 1973c. M.O.S. bluebird project results for 1973. *Maryland Birdlife* 29: 139–143.

————. 1974a. Some facts about incubation. *Purple Martin Capital News* 9 (5): 8–9.

————. 1974b. Bluebird nesting box project 1974. *Atlantic Naturalist* 29: 163–165.

————. 1975. Bluebird nesting box project 1975. *Atlantic Naturalist* 30: 173–174.

INDEX